"Ignorance of the Scriptures is ignorance of Christ."

St. Jerome
Prologue to Isaiah

de-coding
DA VINCI

de-coding DA VINCI

*The facts behind
the fiction of*
The Da Vinci Code

AMY
WELBORN

Our Sunday Visitor Publishing Division
Our Sunday Visitor, Inc.
Huntington, Indiana 46750

Our Sunday Visitor Publishing Division
Our Sunday Visitor, Inc.
200 Noll Plaza
Huntington, IN 46750

ISBN: 1-59276-101-1 (Inventory No. T153)
LCCN: 2004102144

Cover design by Eric Schoening.
Cover art courtesy of Scala/Art Resource, NY: Leonardo da Vinci (1452-1519). *The Vitruvian Man*, ca. 1492. Drawing. Accademia, Venice, Italy. Interior design by Sherri L. Hoffman.

PRINTED IN THE UNITED STATES OF AMERICA

CONTENTS

PREFACE

In the spring of 2003, Doubleday released a novel called *The Da Vinci Code* by Dan Brown.

Supported by an unusually intense pre-publication marketing campaign, *The Da Vinci Code* took off and, after a little more than a year, had sold almost six million hardback copies, and will soon be coming to a theater near you in a film directed by Ron Howard (*Apollo 13*, *A Beautiful Mind*).

The shelves of your local bookstore are crowded with suspense thrillers, but there seems to be something different about *The Da Vinci Code* — it's got people talking in a way that novels by James Patterson or John Grisham don't. What's going on?

Well, to tell the absolute truth, the first thing that's going on here is brilliant marketing. It's important to be aware that these days, if a particular product is surrounded by a "buzz," most of the time that's because a company has worked hard to create that buzz, as Doubleday did with this book well before its publication.

But there's more, of course. Once people started reading *The Da Vinci Code*, they couldn't help but wonder about some of the puzzling assertions author Dan Brown makes in the novel:

- Did Leonardo da Vinci really use his art to communicate secret knowledge about the Holy Grail?
- Is it true that the Gospels don't tell the true story of Jesus?
- Were Jesus and Mary Magdalene married?
- Did Jesus really designate Mary Magdalene as the leader of his movement, not Peter?

What seems to intrigue readers is that the characters in *The Da Vinci Code* have answers to these questions, and they are expressed in the book as factually based, supported by the work and opinions of historians and other researchers. Brown even cites real books as sources within the novel. Readers are naturally wondering why they've not heard of these ideas before. They're also wondering, if what Brown says is true, what the implications for their faith could be. After all, if the Gospels are false accounts, isn't all of Christianity as we know it a lie?

This book is intended to help you unpack all of this and to explore the truth behind *The Da Vinci Code*. We'll look at Brown's sources and see if they're trustworthy witnesses to history. We'll ask if his characterization of early Christian writings, teaching, and disputes — events that are widely documented and have been studied for hundreds of years by intelligent, open-minded people — are accurate. We'll look at Jesus and Mary Magdalene — the people at the center of this novel — and see if anything at all that *The Da Vinci Code* has to say about them is based on historical record. And along the way, we'll find a startling number of blatant, glaring errors on matters great and small that should send up red flags to anyone reading the novel as a source of facts, rather than just pure fiction.

In *The Da Vinci Code*, we're constantly reminded that things just might not really be as they seem.

Read this book with an open mind; you'll find out how very true that is.

HOW TO USE THIS BOOK

You need not have read *The Da Vinci Code* to benefit from reading this book. A detailed plot synopsis is provided so you can understand the major issues the novel raises in order to be more informed as you discuss it with others.

In *De-coding Da Vinci*, I've addressed the most frequent questions readers of the novel have asked, particularly about theological and historical issues. Throughout the book, you will also find boxed material that corrects and clarifies many of the lesser errors and inaccuracies contained in *The Da Vinci Code*.

This book is useful for individuals as well as for groups. Review and discussion questions are provided at the end of each chapter.

The specific claims of *The Da Vinci Code* work to a bigger purpose in this book. Examining them gives us a chance to revisit basic Christian teaching about Jesus' identity and ministry, the history of the early Church, the role of women in religion, and the connection between apostolic faith and our faith today. Whether you have read *The Da Vinci Code* or not, I hope you find in this book an opportunity to grow in understanding of the historical roots of authentic Christian faith.

INTRODUCTION

The Da Vinci Code incorporates elements attractive to many readers: suspense, secrets, a puzzle, a hint of romance, and the suspicion that the world is not as it seems, and the Powers That Be don't want you to know The Truth That's Out There.

The novel begins as Robert Langdon, a Harvard professor of "religious symbology" (there is no such field, by the way), visiting Paris, is called to the scene of a crime in the Louvre. A curator, one Jacques Saunière, revered as an expert on the goddess and the "sacred feminine," lies dead — presumably murdered — in one of the galleries.

Before his death, it seems that Saunière had time enough to arrange himself on the floor in the position of Leonardo da Vinci's drawing of *The Vitruvian Man* — the famous image of a human figure, limbs extended, within a circle — as well as leave some other clues involving numbers, anagrams, and a pentagram, drawn on his body with his own blood.

In time, Sophie Neveu, a cryptologist who is also Saunière's granddaughter, is dispatched to the scene. She had received a call from him earlier, begging her to come see him, be reconciled, and learn something important about her family. Sophie is able to interpret the clues her grandfather has left, have several conversations with Langdon about goddess worship, find a Very Important Key he has left her, behind another Leonardo painting, and . . . we're off.

Who killed Saunière? What secret was he keeping? What does he want Sophie to understand? Why is an albino "monk" from Opus Dei trying to kill everyone? The rest of the novel, encompassing four hundred fifty-four pages, one hundred five chapters, but, amazingly, somehow covering a time span of a little more than a single day, takes us to various European points, along with Langdon and Sophie, seeking the answer, which is, quite simply this:

(Sorry to spoil the plot, but it's got to be done.)

Saunière was a Grand Master of a shadowy secret group called the "Priory of Sion," which was dedicated to the cause of preserving the truth about Jesus, Mary Magdalene, and, by extension, the entire human race.

Humanity, as we are told in the book, originally and for millennia, practiced a spirituality that was balanced between the masculine and the feminine, in which goddesses and the power of women were revered.

This was what Jesus was about. He lived and preached a message of peace, love, and human unity, and, to embody the message, he took Mary Magdalene as his wife and entrusted the leadership of this movement to her. She was pregnant with their child when he was crucified.

Peter, jealous of Mary's role, led his own end of the movement gathered around Jesus, one dedicated to repressing and replacing Jesus' real teaching with his own, and supplanting Mary Magdalene with himself as leader of this movement.

Mary was forced to flee to France, where she eventually died. Her and Jesus' offspring were the root of the Merovingian royal line in France, and she and the "sacred feminine" that she embodies — not any material cup — are the real "Holy Grail."

Were the Merovingian royal family the founders of Paris, as Brown says? (see *DVC*, p. 257). Not even close. Paris was established by a tribe of Celtic Gauls called the Parisii in the third century B.C. What the Merovingians did was to make Paris the capital of the Frankish kingdom in A.D. 508.

So, the history of the past two thousand years is, underneath all of the events recorded in the history books (by the "winners," of course), a history of the struggle between the Catholic Church (not Christianity as a whole, mind you, but the Catholic Church) and the Priory of Sion. The Church, through its establishment of the Canon of Scripture, doctrinal statements, and even treatment of women, has worked to suppress the truth about the Holy Grail and, by extension, the "sacred feminine," while the Knights Templar and the Priory of Sion struggled to protect the Grail (Mary's bones), her bloodline, and the devotion to the "sacred feminine."

Saunière had guarded this knowledge, knowledge that Leonardo da Vinci, a member of the Priory himself, had embedded throughout his work. Saunière had a personal stake it in as well — he, and therefore his granddaughter Sophie, were of that Merovingian line. But Sophie, of course, knew none of this, and had even become distanced from her grandfather years ago when she stumbled into a secret room in his country home and discovered him and a woman, in the midst of a crowd of masked, chanting onlookers, having some sort of ecstatic ritual sex.

Of course, by the end, we understand that this woman was her grandmother, and all she and Gramps were doing in that room was keeping the faith alive. We also learn that the "Grail" — Mary Magdalene's remains and documents proving the bloodline — are buried within I. M. Pei's glittering, glass, seventy-foot pyramid that stands as a new entrance to the Louvre, where, at the end of the novel, Langdon falls to his knees in reverence, hearing, he thinks, the wisdom of ages, in a woman's voice, coming to him from the earth.

Nothing New Under the Sun

Much of the foundation for *The Da Vinci Code's* plot might seem new and intricately creative, but the harsh truth is that most of it isn't new at all.

Quite simply, what Brown has done here is weave a number of different strands of speculation, esoteric lore, and pseudo-history published in other books, cramming them all onto the pages of his novel. If you're at all familiar with these other books, it's actually rather shocking how much in the novel is simply lifted from them.

Brown provides a bibliography on his website, and cites a few of these books in the novel itself. His sources fall into three basic categories:

1) *Holy Blood, Holy Grail* and its bloodline. This book, written by Michael Baigent, Richard Leigh, and Henry Lincoln, was published in 1981, and was the basis of a British Broadcasting Corporation television program. Marketed as nonfiction, it is widely derided as a work of speculation, unfounded assumptions, and is based on fraudulent documents. The authors were, at the time of the book's publication, a teacher with a psychology degree, a novelist, and a television producer, respectively.

Another title in this genre is *The Templar Revelation*, by Lynn Picknett and Clive Prince, experts in the paranormal, who also have *The Mammoth Book of UFOs* to their credit.

The entire Jesus-Mary Magdalene-Holy Grail-Priory of Sion element of *The Da Vinci Code* is derived from these two books.

2) The "sacred feminine." Since the nineteenth century, some have speculated about a lost age of the goddess, during which the "sacred feminine" was reverenced, a period that was supplanted by a war-mongering patriarchy. In more recent years, some writers have melded this thinking with their images of Mary Magdalene. An American named Margaret Starbird has made this her particular crusade in several books. Brown's presentation of Mary Magdalene is highly dependent on Starbird's work, especially *The Woman With the Alabaster Jar*, which Starbird herself describes as "fiction."

3) Gnosticism. As we will see later, "Gnosticism" was an intellectual and spiritual system widespread in the ancient world. It has many facets, but in short, most forms of Gnostic thinking were esoteric (true knowledge was available to only a few — the word

"gnosis" means "knowledge") and anti-material (they viewed the corporeal world, including the body, as evil).

There are some writings from the second through fifth centuries that are clearly syntheses of Gnostic and Christian thinking. Scholars have varying opinions of these writings, but most date them far later than the Gospels, with — and this is important — *little, if any, direct independent insight into the actual words and deeds of Jesus.* Brown ignores this view, preferring to rely on the work of a tiny minority of scholars and other non-scholarly writers who believe that Gnostic writings do reflect the reality of the earliest movement gathered around Jesus. It is on these works that Brown bases his descriptions of what Jesus "really" taught.

These sources should send up red flags right away. There's not one serious work of Christian history on his bibliography — not a single work of significant New Testament scholarship, or even the standard reference volumes that any undergraduate reading up on early Christian history would be expected to use. He doesn't even cite the New Testament itself as a source for early Christian history.

One of the points Brown often makes in interviews is that his work is partly about recovering lost history that has been suppressed. He likes to assert that history is "written by the winners." This means that if you see historical events as a struggle between forces, the victors are the ones who will leave records, and it's their version of history that will survive. The sources he uses purport to present this "lost history." There is a kernel of truth to this perspective, of course. History can never be presented in a thoroughly objective way, for human beings aren't thoroughly objective. We always see and relate events through the prism of perspective. Everyone involved in a car accident has a slightly different version of events, for example.

But that doesn't mean the accident itself *didn't happen.*

While observers of an accident might be unsure as to the exact events leading up to it, and the victim might certainly have a different story than the driver at fault, there is no doubt there *was* an accident, nor is there any doubt that, despite the limitations of the observers, there is, indeed, an objective truth as to who caused the accident, no matter how difficult it may be to unearth.

The same is true of the historical record. It is true that up to recent times, for example, the conquest of the West was told from the European perspective, the "winners." In recent years, scholars have tried to tell the other side of the story, that of the native peoples, whose perspective on the conquest was obviously different. There's no doubt, then, that there is more to the picture of the European conquest of North America than the conquerors say, than the native peoples say, or that any one of us can completely understand. What's still true, though, is that the conquest *happened* out of certain motives and with particular consequences which, if we have the right information, can be perceived, even as they are interpreted differently.

However, in *The Da Vinci Code*, Brown uses "history is written by the winners" to suggest that the whole history of Christianity, beginning with Jesus himself, *is a lie*, written by those who were determined to suppress Jesus' "real" message. It's not about differing interpretations of Jesus' life and message. It's about the basic data itself: that what we read in the New Testament and what records of early Christianity itself exist, aren't accurate presentations of what really happened.

In the novel, the scholar Sir Leigh Teabing says point blank that "heretics" in early Christianity — those who are represented by the Gnostic writings Brown cites — are those who remained faithful to "the original history of Christ" (p. 234).

That's really the bottom line here, and that's a serious charge. We're going to spend the rest of this book examining these assertions in more detail, but it's still important to lay out the basic framework right up front so we see what's at stake.

Brown claims that Jesus wanted the movement that followed him to be about a greater awareness of the "sacred feminine." He says that this movement, under the leadership and inspiration of Mary Magdalene, thrived during the first three centuries until it was brutally suppressed by the Emperor Constantine.

There's no evidence to suggest that this is true. It didn't happen.

Certainly, there was diversity in early Christianity. There is no doubt there were intense discussions about who Jesus was and what he meant. There is also strong evidence that, in certain communities, women held leadership roles in Christianity — such as deaconess — that eventually died out (and were revived in later forms of Christianity, incidentally).

But you really have to understand that none of this diversity, change, or development in early Christian history occurred in the way *The Da Vinci Code* suggests it did. When early Christian leaders sought to affirm the truth of Christian teaching, their criterion was not about gender or power. It was, as we can see from their own writings, if we bother to read them, about faithfulness to what Jesus said and did.

There may be a lot about early Christianity we don't know or aren't sure of. These are issues that have been freely and openly debated by serious scholars for years, and sometimes, even two thousand years after the events, new evidence comes to light that expands the picture we have.

However, nowhere in any of that serious scholarly work do you find anyone taking seriously the suggestion that Jesus' mission was all about sending forth Mary Magdalene to carry his message of the "sacred feminine."

Credible sources simply don't even hint at such a thing. Credible scholarly sources also suggest that much of Brown's other assertions — about everything from the nature of the Grail myth to the Priory of Sion to the role of goddess worship in the ancient world — just aren't supported by the evidence that's out there.

And, as we'll see as we plow through this novel, there are many other bizarre, outlandish, and error-filled claims. From statements made about the geography of Paris to those on the life of

Leonardo da Vinci himself, there's no reason to view this book as a halfway reliable source on *any* field of study except, perhaps, cryptography.

"Relax, It's Only a Novel"

The Da Vinci Code has created quite a stir, and along with the stir are calls to just relax and let the whole thing blow over. I hear it all the time.

"It's only a novel," some folks say. "Everyone knows it's fiction. So why not just enjoy it on that level?"

Well, there are several reasons why we can't do that. First, there is no such thing as "only a novel." Culture matters. Culture communicates. We should always be interested in the content of culture and its impact on us, no matter if we're talking about art, film, music, or writing.

But, even more specifically, the author of this particular book suggests that there really is more at work here than just imagination, and he encourages his readers to accept certain problematic assertions about history as factual.

There is, of course, a long history — dating back to the earliest days of Christianity — of interweaving the known facts about Jesus with imaginative stories, comparable to the Jewish tradition of "midrash." Legends about the Holy Family, for example, abound, like that which says that the rosemary plant received its sweet smell as a reward after Mary spread out her cloak to dry on a rosemary bush during the flight to Egypt.

Christian art through the ages is filled with interesting and often illuminating details that have no basis in the words of Scripture or early Christian tradition. And, in more recent decades, fiction writers have done their fair share of using the story of Jesus as a basis for novels: *The Robe* by Lloyd C. Douglas, and *The Silver Chalice* by Thomas Costain, are just two very popular examples among many, the latter dealing, incidentally, with the Holy Grail.

Historical fiction is a very popular genre, but in writing historical fiction, the author makes an implicit deal with the reader. He or she promises that, while the novel concerns fictional characters engaged in imagined activities, the basic historical framework is correct. In fact, many people enjoy reading historical fiction because it's an entertaining, painless way to learn history. They trust that the author is telling the truth about history.

The Da Vinci Code is different. In all of these other examples, everyone from the artist to the viewer or reader understands the difference between known facts and imaginative details, and buys into a basic responsibility to and expectation of historical reliability, when it applies. In *The Da Vinci Code*, imaginative detail and false historical assertions are presented as facts and the fruit of serious historical research, which they simply are not.

As we noted in the last chapter, Brown presents a lengthy bibliography of works he used in the writing of the novel, all of which have a historical veneer to them, even if most of them are not real history.

In the front of the book, Brown presents a list of facts contained in his novel. He states that the Priory of Sion and Opus Dei are both real organizations. He ends his declaration by saying:

"All descriptions of artwork, architecture, documents, and secret rituals in this novel are accurate."

He does not explicitly include "declarations about Christian origins" in his list, but it is implicit in his inclusion of "documents." More importantly, all of Brown's assertions about Christian origins are put in the mouths of his scholar characters — Langdon and Teabing, in particular, who often quote from real contemporary works and frame their statements in phrases such as, "Historians marvel that . . ." and "Fortunately for historians . . ." and "Many scholars claim. . . ."

These discussions function as a device for communicating the ideas from *Holy Blood, Holy Grail*, Margaret Starbird, or who knows where else, to the reader, and communicating them in a way that implies they are factual, accepted by "historians" and "scholars" worldwide.

Moreover, Brown has been rather up front in interviews about his method and purpose. He has repeatedly stated that he is delighted to be sharing these findings with readers because he wants to participate in the telling of this "lost history." In other words, in his interviews, Brown suggests that part of what he's trying to do in *The Da Vinci Code* is teach a little history:

"Two thousand years ago, we lived in a world of Gods and Goddesses. Today we live in a world solely of Gods. Women in most cultures have been stripped of their spiritual power. The novel touches on questions of how and why this shift occurred . . . and on what lessons we might learn from it regarding our future" (www.danbrown.com).

And, to a startling extent, readers are accepting these theories as facts. One need only read reader reviews of the book on Amazon.com, or peruse the many newspaper stories about the impact of the book, to see how true this is. Perhaps you have even encountered reactions like this among your own family and friends, which is why you started reading this book in the first place.

So no, it's not "just a novel." *The Da Vinci Code* purports to teach history within the framework of fiction. Let's take a look at the lesson plan.

one

SECRETS AND LIES

*T*he *Da Vinci Code* is all about secrets: secret societies, secret knowledge, secret documents, and even family secrets.

The most important secrets, of course, concern Jesus and Mary Magdalene. Brown's characters frequently assert that the traditional Christian understanding of Jesus' life and ministry is false. Which would mean, then, that the New Testament, the source of that understanding, is a completely untrustworthy source of information.

That's it. There's no way of getting around it. Be intrigued by the possibilities if you like, but giving any credence to any of the historical claims of *The Da Vinci Code* means, to follow things to their logical end, a rejection of the account that the New Testament gives of Jesus, his ministry, and the early days of Christianity.

Is that a reasonable stance? Could the New Testament really be so useless, or worse — a deception?

Let's consider this, too: Are the sources that Brown uses really superior to the New Testament as sources about Jesus?

For example, all of those other "gospels" Brown's characters are always talking about, those secret writings: Should you believe that they tell the truth about Jesus just because he says they do? Let's see.

Gnostic Gospels

As we've noted before, Brown derives his ideas about Jesus, Mary, and the Holy Grail from pseudo-history books such as *Holy Blood, Holy Grail* and *The Templar Revelation*. Yet, when he's describing what he says is the real nature of Jesus' mission and Mary Magdalene's role in it, he turns to other sources.

In particular, on page 235 and following, his historian, Teabing, uses books referred to as *The Gnostic Gospels* as evidence for the tale he is weaving about Jesus. He says they speak of "Christ's ministry in very human terms," and he quotes passages describing a close relationship between Jesus and Mary Magdalene, as well as the apostles' jealousy of that relationship.

Teabing explains that all of this reveals Mary's real role as the pre-eminent recipient and apostle of Jesus' wisdom teaching, and sets the stage for the conflict between her and Peter, which then flows neatly into the other theories lifted from the other books.

But do these writings live up to the hype? Should we trust them to give us the truth about Jesus' life, message, and ministry? And is the Jesus presented in them really as charmingly "human" as Brown claims?

These "Gnostic Gospels," as they are called, are certainly real documents. They are, indeed, centuries old, mostly not gospels, strictly speaking, and are the fruit of a diffuse, hard-to-define movement that was very popular throughout the ancient world during the second and third centuries, and for several hundred years afterward.

Gnosticism was not an organized movement. There were some clearly distinct Gnostic sects, but Gnostic ways of thinking and concepts crept into other intellectual systems of the period. You might compare it to the impact of the self-help and self-esteem movement over the past twenty years of American life. Wherever you look, it seems, you hear admonitions to "be your best self" and to put self-improvement at the center of your priorities. You find it embodied in television programs and films, in music, in business practices, in education, and even in churches. It's not organized, it has no central leadership, it manifests itself in different ways, some more explicit than others, but it's clearly there.

Gnostic thinking, while taking different forms in different places and times, usually involved a few consistent themes:

- The source of goodness, of authentic life, is the spiritual.
- The material and corporeal world is evil.
- The plight of humanity is the imprisonment of a spiritual "spark" inside the prison of a material body.
- Salvation — or release of this imprisoned spirit — is achieved by attaining knowledge (remember: "gnosis" *means* "knowledge").
- Only a few are worthy to receive this secret knowledge.

There are endless variations of Gnostic thinking in the ancient world, some involving quite elaborate hierarchies of reality and intricate rituals.

Inevitably, Gnostic elements found their way into the thinking of some Christians (just as self-help language has crept into the way we talk about our faith). During the second and third centuries, Gnosticism was particularly attractive, and presented Christian thinkers with their first real theological challenge. Gnostic versions of Christianity usually denigrated the Old Testament, de-emphasized or denied the humanity of Jesus, and ignored his Passion and crucifixion.

Gnostics wrote about their beliefs, attracted followers, and engaged in teaching and secret rituals. For nine years during his young adulthood, the great St. Augustine was a member of a Gnostic sect called the Manichaeans, which he eventually left after

Against heresies: Some second- and third-century works that provide insight into the Christian response to Gnosticism, easily available in libraries or on the Internet, are *Against Heresies* by Irenaeus, *Against Marcion* by Tertullian, and *Refutation of All Heresies* by Hippolytus.

honestly confronting the inconsistencies and absurdities of Manichaean teaching (see *Confessions,* Books 3-5).

The writings Brown uses to paint his picture of what Jesus was really like were written by adherents of Gnostic versions of Christianity. This thinking flourished during the second and third centuries, which means, then, that these writings, which are supposed to reveal secret, authentic knowledge about Jesus, come from the same period — more than *a hundred years after* Jesus' ministry, far later than any of the New Testament books, which were all composed by the end of the first century.

So, with an honest and open mind, we have to wonder, without even examining their content (which we'll do later), why in the world we should believe that these *later* documents tell us more about events than *earlier* documents?

The "Other" Gospels

Now let's look at two of the documents Brown's characters give special attention to: *The Gospel of Philip* and *The Gospel of Mary,* from which Teabing reads passages indicating that Jesus and Mary Magdalene had an intimate, unique relationship of which the other apostles were jealous.

The Gospel of Philip was one of the documents discovered at Nag Hammadi, in Egypt, in 1945. The astonishing find, sealed in a jar, was composed of a library, excluding duplicates, of 45 different titles. Written in Coptic (the Egyptian language rendered in Greek letters), copied by anonymous monks, the works almost all incorporated some Gnostic elements, and some clearly reflect Gnostic Christian beliefs. Based on dates on some of the covers, scholars believe that these documents were written in the mid- to late-fourth century, although many of the original works, of which these are copies, are certainly earlier.

Although not much earlier. As Philip Jenkins notes in his book *The Hidden Gospels,* the standard scholarly dating for *The Gospel of Philip,* from which Teabing reads a passage referring to Mary as

Brown says that the Nag Hammadi texts were on "scrolls" — they most certainly were not. They were codices, an early form of book.

Jesus' "companion," is, at the earliest, A.D. 250. That's two hundred years after Jesus' ministry. It may be called a "gospel," but it has hardly any material in common with any of the Gospels, and, like most of the Gnostic materials, is completely different in style. The canonical Gospels have a clear, strong narrative, and highlight Jesus' Passion, crucifixion and resurrection. The *Gospel of Philip* is a meandering, disjointed collection of sayings in dialogue form that are clearly reflective of Gnostic thinking.

The same can be said for *The Gospel of Mary*, also a Nag Hammadi text. It is shorter than *Philip*, and has a bit more of a plot, if you want to think of it that way. Jesus speaks to the disciples, then leaves. Mary Magdalene seeks to lift their hearts by sharing some of the knowledge Jesus has given her, knowledge that is well-received by some of the apostles and questioned by others. We will look at this document more closely in a later chapter, but here we are concerned with its value as a source of information about Jesus' life and teaching.

Part of what Mary Magdalene describes in this document is the ascent of the soul through various levels of life after death. This strongly reflects Gnostic thinking of the late second century, and for this reason the vast majority of scholars date it from that period, at the earliest.

Brown has Teabing assert that these Nag Hammadi documents, as well as the Dead Sea Scrolls, tell the "true Grail story." This is, frankly, odd. Two of the forty-five Nag Hammadi texts describe a unique, but by no means unambiguously marital, Mary Magdalene-Jesus relationship, as a way of fleshing out Gnostic teachings, but there's no mention of any other details of the "Grail story" he says they tell. Further, the Dead Sea Scrolls (discovered in 1947, not in the 1950s as Brown says) don't even contain Christian texts *at all*. They're texts left by an ascetic, monastic Jewish sect called the Essenes. Jesus, Mary Magdalene, and the Grail are, sadly, not mentioned.

Here's what we can make of these Gnostic writings: They are valuable for what they reveal about Gnostic-Christian hybrids of the second century and later. They tell us how these communities used the story of Jesus found in the Synoptic Gospels (Matthew, Mark, and Luke, widely circulated by the beginning of the second century) and shaped it to their own ends, and they might even tell us a bit about the conflicts within those communities.

However, one thing they *don't* offer is any independent, unique information about Jesus of Nazareth and his earliest followers.

Scripture scholar John P. Meier sums up the general scholarly consensus in his book *A Marginal Jew*, when he writes:

"What we see in these later documents is . . . the reaction to or reworking of NT writings by . . . Gnostic Christians developing a mystic speculative system. Their versions of Jesus' words and deeds can be included in a 'corpus of Jesus material' if that corpus is understood to contain simply everything and anything that any ancient source ever identified as coming from Jesus. But such a corpus is the Matthean dragnet (see Matthew 13:47-48) from which the good fish of early tradition must be selected for the containers of serious historical research, while the bad fish of later conflation and invention are tossed back into the murky sea of the uncritical mind. . . . We have been sitting on the beach, sorting the dragnet and throwing the *agrapha,* apocryphal gospels, and the *Gospel of Thomas* back into the sea" (p. 140).

So, back into the murky sea with the "gospels" of Philip, Mary and Thomas. They simply are not useful for trying to understand Jesus' ministry and the shape of very early Christianity.

For Further Reading

The Hidden Gospels: How the Search for Jesus Lost Its Way, by Philip Jenkins, Oxford University Press, 2001.

Questions for Review

1. What was Gnosticism?
2. Why are the Gnostic gospels unreliable sources for information about Jesus?

Questions for Discussion

1. What traces of Gnostic-type thinking do you see in the world today?
2. Why do you think some might be attracted to what the Gnostic writings say about Jesus instead of what the Gospels say?

two

WHO PICKED THE GOSPELS?

If you're going to learn your early Christian history from *The Da Vinci Code,* here's the lesson for today:

Jesus was a wise, mortal teacher, about whose life there were many — "thousands" (p. 234) — of accounts during those first centuries. More than eighty gospels, in fact. But only four were chosen for inclusion in the Bible! By the Emperor Constantine in 325!

Then, in the aftermath of the Council of Nicaea, *The Da Vinci Code* announces, those "thousands" of works that described Jesus' life as a human teacher were suppressed, out of raw political motivation, and, as Langdon says, those who stuck with the mortal-teacher-Jesus story, which he says was the "original history of Christ," were called "heretics" (p. 234).

Up to this point, we've tried really hard to maintain a measured, objective tone in our treatment, but right here the limit has been reached, and we cannot go on.

This is so wrong, it's beyond wrong. It's a fantasy, and not even the most secular scholar and the most non-religious university possible would give any support to Brown's account of the formation of the New Testament.

It's not serious history, so don't be taken in by it. Do look at this weird construction of the past as yet one more big warning sign against even starting to view any of what's between the pages of this novel as factual. And do use it as an opportunity to learn the far more interesting story of how the New Testament really came to be.

Not Such a Shocking Development

In *The Da Vinci Code*, scholar Teabing apparently stuns Sophie when he announces, "The Bible did not arrive by fax from heaven" (p. 231). This is supposed to be stunning news, against which his account of what "really happened" is contrasted.

The implication is that if the Bible did, indeed, not arrive by fax, complete, bound, and with a handy table of contents written by God, the only alternative scenario remaining is that the formation of the Scriptures was a process in which scores of equally valid accounts of Jesus' life were either accepted or discarded by people motivated by the desire for power.

Well, that's simply not what happened.

Be assured that the process — establishing the canon of the Scriptures — is no secret. One could get a book out of the library and get the full story in a matter of minutes. Moreover, human involvement doesn't diminish the sacredness of the books.

After all, Jesus didn't exactly leave a Bible behind when he ascended into heaven. He left a Church — the apostles, Mary, his mother, and other disciples, including both men and women. As essential as the Bible is to Christians, as fundamental and sure a source of revelation, it's good, if a little startling, to remember that during those first decades, Christians lived, learned, and worshiped as Christians — without the New Testament. They had learned their faith by reflecting on the Old Testament, and by way of oral teaching, rooted in the apostles' witness. This faith was shaped and nourished through encounters with the living Lord in baptism, the Lord's Supper, the forgiveness of sins, and shared life with other Christians.

Out of this Church — the Body nourished by the Living Lord — came the books of the New Testament, the testimony of witnesses to Jesus eventually written down, winnowed, and defined.

No fax from heaven? Not a problem. Maybe it was big news to poor Sophie, but it's not news to us.

Sayings and Stories

From the very beginning, certain Christian texts were valued above others.

They were prized for several reasons: They had origins in the apostolic era; they authentically preserved the words and deeds of Jesus; they could be used in liturgies, preaching, and teaching to accurately communicate the fullness of faith in Jesus to the entire Christian community.

Please note the absence of "addresses the sacred feminine" or "denigrates women's power" in this list.

Anyway, by the mid-second century, Christians were already placing this kind of value, rooted in what was coming to be called the "rule of faith" on two major sets of writing: The Gospels of Matthew, Mark, Luke, and John, and the letters of Paul.

How do we know that these works were valued? Because they were read in worship and referenced by the writings of Christian teachers that have come down to us.

It's really important to note that, despite what Brown says, there were not eighty gospels in circulation. That number has absolutely no basis in fact.

Sure, there were other gospels in existence beside the four in our New Testament. Luke says as much in the beginning of his own work:

"Inasmuch as many have undertaken to compile a narrative of the things which have been accomplished among us . . . it seemed good to me also, having followed all things closely for some time past, to write an orderly account for you, most excellent Theophilus,

Gospel: "Gospel" literally means "good news." The Gospel is the Good News of our salvation through Jesus Christ. Gospels are written records of that Good News.

that you may know the truth concerning the things of which you have been informed" (Luke 1:1, 3).

Scholars believe that collections of Jesus' sayings provided one of the sources for the Gospels, and there are a few gospels — *The Gospel of Peter, The Gospel of the Egyptians,* and *The Gospel of the Hebrews* — that were in limited use.

The fact is that even by the middle of the second century, the Gospels of Matthew, Mark, Luke, and John were the primary sources that Christians used in proclaiming the story of Jesus in worship and teaching.

Just as interesting is another category of writings that Christian communities read in their worship, long before the Gospels were written: the letters of Paul.

It's true. The earliest written New Testament books were the letters of Paul, perhaps 1 Thessalonians, written around the year A.D. 50. Paul became a follower of Christ, but two or three years after Jesus' death and resurrection, and spent the rest of his life traveling, establishing Christian communities all around the Mediterranean, and, we believe, dying as a martyr in Rome. He wrote many letters to those communities he founded, and, over time, those communities started making copies of the letters and send-

> Teabing describes a "legendary 'Q' *Document*," Jesus' teachings, perhaps written in his own hand, that the "Vatican" even admits exists (p. 256). The truth about "Q" isn't so shocking. There is a great deal of shared material between Matthew and Luke, not in Mark. Scholars hypothesize that they might have used a common source document, which they called "Q," for *quelle,* the German word for "source." The Vatican — along with most other people — is perfectly comfortable with its possible existence.

ing them off to other Christians. In fact, a collection of Paul's letters was already in circulation among Christians by the end of the first century.

Now, let's step back and see what we have so far.

From very early on, the accounts of Jesus' life, which eventually were gathered into the four Gospels we have today, were circulated among Christians and received as accurate accounts of his life, and an authentic point of contact with the living Christ. Many of Paul's letters were circulated as well. They were used, along with Old Testament texts, in worship. Christian writers quoted from them. The story they told of Jesus — as the One whom God had sent to reconcile the world, who had suffered, died, rose, and still lives as Lord — was the story that shaped early Christian thinking, worship, and life.

There were, to be perfectly blunt about it, no "thousands" of documents existing "chronicling His life as a *mortal* man," nor were there eighty other gospels that, as Teabing says, "were considered" for inclusion, as if there were a stack of codices and scrolls on a committee's meeting table. That we can safely say.

There is absolutely no doubt that when it comes to the Gospels (which are our primary concern), the four Gospels we have today were considered normative by the Christian community by the middle of the second century. Christian writers such as Justin Martyr, Tertullian, and Irenaeus, all writing and teaching during this time in, respectively, Rome, North Africa, and Lyons (in what is now France), all reference the four Gospels we know now as primary sources of information about Jesus.

Quite simply, Constantine didn't do it.

"Countless Translations, Additions, and Revisions"

In his lecture on Bible history, after he announces that the Scriptures did not arrive by fax, Teabing alerts Sophie to the "countless translations, additions, and revisions. History has never had a definitive version of the book" (p. 231).

Well, okay, if by "definitive" you mean "absolutely original texts written in the hand of their authors."

Again, this is what we call a "straw man": a point raised in an argument that no one believes anyway.

There are, indeed, many manuscripts of New Testament books and portions of books. More than five thousand are from the early centuries of Christianity, the earliest dating from A.D. 125-130, with more than thirty, dating from the late second or early third centuries, which contain "good chunks of entire books and two which cover most of the gospels and Acts or letters of Paul" (Craig Blomberg in *Reasonable Faith*, by William Lane Craig, p. 194).

These manuscripts are, of course, marked by minor variations, but here's what's important to note:

"The only textual variants which affect more than a sentence or two (and most affect only individual words or phrases) are John 7:53-8:11 and Mark 16:9-20. . . . But overall, 97-99% of the NT can be reconstructed beyond any reasonable doubt" (*Reasonable Faith*, p. 194).

Now, if this bothers you, consider this:

"For Caesar's *Gallic War* (ca. 50 B.C.), there are only nine or ten good manuscripts, and the oldest dates from nine hundred years after the events it records. Only thirty-five of Livy's one hundred forty-two books of Roman history survive, in about twenty manuscripts, only one of which is as old as the fourth century [Livy lived from ca. 64 B.C.-ca. A.D. 12]. Of Tacitus's fourteen books of Roman history, we have only four and one-half, in two manuscripts dating from the ninth and eleventh centuries. . . . The point is simply that the textual evidence for what the NT authors wrote far outstrips the documentation we have for any other ancient writing. . . . There is absolutely no support for claims that the standard modern editions of the Greek NT do not very closely approximate what the NT writers actually wrote" (ibid).

Christians understand that the Scriptures we have are the results of God working through human vessels. Those human vessels are flawed and limited, but the point is that the manuscript evidence of the New Testament is, in large part, a consistent, ancient record whose manuscript variations do not affect the meaning of the text.

The Formation of the Canon

Now, there were certainly other works besides these circulating among Christian communities and even used in liturgies. There were instructional texts, such as the *Didache* and *The Shepherd of Hermas*. There were other letters from other apostles or those associated with him. The *First Letter of Clement*, written around A.D. 96 from the Church in Rome to the Church in Corinth, was widely read, especially in Egypt and Syria. There were even *a few* other texts with "gospel" in the title that were used by various Christian communities — a *Gospel of the Hebrews, Gospel of the Egyptians,* and *Gospel of Peter,* for example.

Why aren't these in our New Testaments today?

There are reasons, but we need to make it clear up front that those reasons have nothing to do with the political machinations that Brown suggests, and for sure nothing to do with the Council of Nicaea or Constantine. It's also important to point out that these Gnostic texts that Brown puts at the center of his theories were *never* considered canonical by anyone except the Gnostics who produced them.

As happens so many times in Christian history, the move to define the books that were acceptable for use by the Church in worship came as a response to a challenge.

> **Canon:** From a Greek word meaning "rule," the group of books recognized by the Church as inspired by God and authoritative for use by the entire Church.

The challenge, coming in the mid-second century, came from two directions: one movement seeking to drastically reduce the number of books accepted as Scripture, and the other to add to it.

The first challenge was from a man named Marcion. Marcion, the son of a bishop who, incidentally, excommunicated him, organized a movement in Rome around his beliefs that, among other points, deplored the God described in the Old Testament. He taught that the only valid Scriptures for Christians were ten of Paul's letters and an edited version of the *Gospel of Luke*.

The second set of challenges came from Gnosticism, which we discussed in the last chapter, and from another heresy called Montanism. These versions of Christianity had their own holy books, as we've seen, and the question naturally arose — what place do they have? Do they represent a valid understanding of Jesus?

The squeeze was coming from both ends: Marcion wanted to remove books; the Gnostics were claiming equal authority for theirs. Obviously, more definition was needed.

Let's clear up one point right now. The need for definition didn't come because people in power felt their positions threatened. During this period, Christianity was a minority religion, periodically persecuted by Roman authorities, whose adherents risked much — including their lives — to be faithful to faith in Christ.

It may puzzle some to hear that Marcion was the son of a bishop, especially those who are tempted to accept Brown's assertion that early Christianity was inimical to marriage and sexuality. In Eastern Christianity, both Catholic and Orthodox priests may marry. This tradition goes back to antiquity, when some clerics were celibate and others were married. St. Patrick of Ireland, for example, was the son of a deacon and the grandson of a priest.

There were no bonus points for remaining faithful to the Gospel. If anything, it was the opposite.

No, the need for definition came because the consequences of accepting either Marcion or the Gnostics' understanding of Christianity were grave. Both, in their own way, represented a far different and diminished explanation of Jesus and his teaching. Both cut Christianity off from its Jewish roots, and Gnosticism, in particular, stripped Jesus of his humanity. No Gnostic-Christian writings include accounts of Jesus' Passion and death. Both presented visions of Jesus that were profoundly at odds with the picture that is painted in Christians' earliest recollections of him, recorded in the four Gospels, in Paul, and in the ongoing life of the Church.

In response to these challenges, Christian leaders began to define more clearly the books appropriate for use by Christian churches in liturgy and teaching. For a couple of centuries, this was done through the shared teaching and statements of individual bishops. Outside that commonly accepted core of the Gospels and Pauline epistles, there was still fluidity, though. Some bishops, particularly in the West, thought that the Letter to the Hebrews was not acceptable, and some Eastern bishops were not sure about the Book of Revelation.

The questions, though, were not about the spiritual worth of these works. The questions were always related to the standards implicit in this process since the beginning: Which books best embody the reality of who Jesus was and is for the entire Church? Do these books come from the age of the apostles? Does what they say about Jesus fit what the Gospels tell us? Are these books edifying for the entire Church, or are they of more local interest?

Not, mind you, "Do they tell a secret story about Jesus and Mary Magdalene that we must hide from the world." No. That did not seem to be the problem.

Eventually, as Christianity became more established, and the threat of persecution lifted, Christian leaders were able to meet and make decisions for the broader Church. A council at Laodicea around A.D. 363 confirmed centuries of Church use and reflection by a list of canonical books that included all that we know, but the Book of Revelation. In 393, a council met in Hippo, in North Africa, and established the canon, including the Book of Revelation, that we know today, saying that these were the books that could be read aloud in churches, adding, it's important to note, that on a martyr's feast day, the account of that martyr's passion (suffering and death) could be read as well.

A.D. 363 and A.D. 393. Both dates are several years after Constantine's rule.

In a nutshell, here's the process one more time: The apostles and other disciples are witnesses to Jesus' teaching, ministry, miracles, suffering, death, and resurrection. They preserve what they have seen and heard and pass it on. As texts come to be written down, they are constantly compared to the ancient story the original witnesses told. Eventually, in the face of other teachings that stand in direct opposition to the ancient witnesses, Church leaders draw a line, and say that because of this group of books' ties to the apostles and conformity to the ancient witnesses, they are suitable for use in worship and for passing on faith in Jesus.

No secrets, we might add. There's no hidden knowledge being passed around by bishops under the thumb of the Emperor Constantine. The process was all there, out there in the open, from the original witness to the gradual definition of the canon.

And, no thousands of suppressed accounts of Jesus, or eighty gospels, either. In a novel maybe, but not in fact.

Who Cares?

It may seem like a small point, but it's not, really. Many readers have been disturbed by *The Da Vinci Code's* version of history. It seems to imply that the Bible we have today is the result of Church leaders unfairly rejecting valid accounts of Jesus just because they were threatened by them.

As you've seen, that's not what happened. Yes, human hands played a role in the establishment of the canon, but those decisions weren't motivated by a desire to oppress women or hold on to power. They were grounded in the obligation — very seriously felt — to ensure that Jesus' life and message were accurately and thoroughly preserved for future generations, and, Christians believe, inspired by the Holy Spirit. Sure, there were books that didn't make it. Some didn't make it because they weren't universal in application, or they couldn't be traced back to apostolic times. Others were rejected because they clearly were nothing but attempts to tack Jesus — barely recognizable as the same Jesus we meet in the Gospels and in Paul — onto new philosophies and spiritual movements.

Sound familiar?

For Further Reading

The New Testament Documents: Are They Reliable? by F. F. Bruce and N. T. Wright, Wm. B. Eerdmans Publishing, 2003.

Questions for Review

1. What was the process of establishing the canon of Scripture?
2. What were the criteria used for which books to include?

Questions for Discussion

1. Why do you think it was important to establish a canon of Scripture?
2. How would you explain to someone that even if the Bible didn't "come down in a fax" from God, we can still trust it as God's authoritative Word?
3. What was the role of the Church in establishing the canon?

three

DIVINE ELECTION

According to *The Da Vinci Code*, Christianity as we know it today is the work, not of Jesus and his disciples, but of the Emperor Constantine, who reigned over the Roman Empire in the fourth century.

Is this true?

Need we even spell it out? Of course not.

Modern Christianity may certainly be diverse, but at the core of all Christian faith is the belief that Jesus, fully divine and fully human, is the One through whom God reconciles the world — and each one of us — to himself, and that salvation (sharing God's life) is found through faith in Jesus, who is not dead, but lives.

Brown, speaking through the characters in his book, would have us believe that this faith is the creation of a fourth-century Roman emperor. In his account (explained by Teabing), here's what happened:

Jesus was revered as a wise human teacher. Writings emphasizing his humanity were widely circulated. Thousands of them, remember. When Constantine came to power, he was distressed by the conflicts between Christianity and paganism, which threatened to divide his Empire. So, he picked Christianity, convened hundreds of bishops at the Council of Nicaea, which he forced to affirm Jesus as Son of God, and that was that.

Honestly, this is so strange. Let's take it apart bit by bit, and then address the crucial question of Jesus' divinity.

Constantine

Constantine (ca. A.D. 272-337) began his reign as Roman emperor in A.D. 306, and solidified his power in A.D. 312, when he defeated

a rival at the famous Battle of Milvian Bridge, supposedly strength-
ened and inspired by a vision he interpreted as Christian.

Exactly what Constantine saw and when he saw it (either before
this battle or another one some time before) is unclear. Some
versions say it was the "chi-rho," the Greek letters "X" and "ρ"
combined — ☧ — which are the first two letters of Christ:
Χριστος. Other accounts say it was a cross.

Up to this point, the practice of Christianity had been essentially illegal in the Roman Empire, and, in fact, Christians had
experienced a particularly vicious, Empire-wide persecution under
the reign of Diocletian just a few years before (A.D. 303-305).

(It would be helpful to pause right here and ask why the Roman
Empire would bother to imprison and torture those who remained
faithful to a wise teacher, if that's all Jesus was? And why would followers of that wise teacher be any kind of threat to the Empire?
There were plenty of philosophical schools and systems floating in
the Empire. They weren't persecuted. Why were Christians?)

For whatever reason — perhaps a faint glimmer of real faith,
the presence of Christians in his own family, or some mysterious
political calculation — one of Constantine's first actions was to
issue an edict of toleration of Christianity, ending persecution for
the moment, at least.

It's true that Constantine, during his reign, extended not only
toleration, but preferences to Christianity. His motives are unclear.
He did want to unify the Empire, which had been seriously
wracked by division and constant conflict for a century. Religion
was certainly a tool in that effort, and perhaps he sensed its
strength and the lessening power of traditional Roman religion.
Perhaps he was influenced by Christian thinkers who had access

to him, and perhaps even by some in his own family, but it does seem that, after a point, Constantine decided to let Christianity be that unifying force.

It is all very strange to us, as accustomed as we are to the separation of church and state, but in the ancient world, there was simply no such thing, in any culture. Every state saw itself as supported, in some way, by divine favor, and with a subsequent responsibility to support religious institutions. Up until Constantine, those religious institutions had been the temples of the Roman gods. When Constantine shifted his interest and support to Christianity, he naturally assumed the same position in relationship to Christian institutions, financing the building of churches and intervening in Church affairs in a way that is startling to us today.

Brown says that Constantine made Christianity the official religion of the Roman Empire. He didn't. He gave strong imperial support to Christianity, but Christianity did not become the official religion of the Roman Empire until the reign of the Emperor Theodosius, who ruled from A.D. 379 to A.D. 395.

The Council of Nicaea

Constantine did, indeed, convene the Council of Nicaea in A.D. 325, in Asia Minor, the land that we now know as Turkey. It was actually the second gathering of bishops he had convened during his reign. Although not all bishops attended, and hardly any from the West, the purpose of the council was to make decisions affecting the entire Church, so it is called an "ecumenical council."

But why? Why did Constantine do this? Well, according to Brown, he did it because he wanted to change Christianity in order to make it more powerful and more effectively suit his purposes.

An ecumenical council is a gathering of bishops from the entire Church. They are named after the places they are held. Catholics recognize twenty-one ecumenical councils, beginning with Nicaea, and ending with the Second Vatican Council (1962-65).

That merely mortal teacher Jesus was of no value to him, but a divine Son of God would be very useful.

We really have to stop and wonder at this. Three hundred bishops gather in Nicaea, bishops who, according to Brown's account, believed that Jesus was a "mortal prophet." Constantine tells them to declare that Jesus is God.

They say — okay. Whatever.

Again, we are moved to say — not quite. Not logical, not what the sources say; quite simply, not what happened.

Why isn't it logical? Oh, perhaps because when you examine what these bishops were up to before they converged on Nicaea — the liturgies they celebrated, the treatises they wrote and used, the Scriptures (well established by then) from which they preached and taught — Jesus as "mortal prophet" is not exactly what you find.

Jesus Is Lord!

Is it true that for three hundred years before Nicaea, what we call "Christianity" was really just about passing around the wisdom of the prophet Jesus?

No. In fact, Christianity never was about that at all.

When we examine the Gospels and Paul's letters, all of which date from the A.D. 50s through about A.D. 95, what we find is a *consistent* pattern of descriptions of Jesus as a human being, in whom God dwelt in a totally unique way.

The Gospels make clear that the apostles did not, at all, understand Jesus' identity before the Resurrection. They are continually confused, mistaken, and, naturally enough, being faithful Jewish men, able to think about Jesus only within the context available to them: as a prophet (yes), teacher, "son of God," and "messiah." In the Jewish context, neither of those latter terms implied a divine nature, implying, rather, a sense of being uniquely chosen by God.

However, in the light of the Resurrection, the apostles finally understood what Jesus had hinted at throughout his ministry and finally explicitly stated, as related in John, chapters 14-17: that he and the Father were one.

If you read the New Testament, you find this expressed in all sorts of ways: You find it in the Gospels; in the memories of Jesus' unique, virginal conception by the Holy Spirit (see Matthew 1-2; Luke 1-2); in all of the accounts of Jesus' baptism and the Trans-figuration; in Jesus' act of forgiving sins, which caused scandal because "only God can forgive sins" (see Luke 7: 36-50; Mark 2:1-12); and in various sayings, scattered through the synoptics and in John, in which Jesus identifies himself with the Father in a way that implies that when we meet Jesus, we encounter God in his mercy and love (see Matthew 10:40; John 14:8-14).

Moving on to the *Acts of the Apostles*, and Paul's letters, which reflect the preaching of the apostles and the early Church, you can't help but run into the conviction, at the center of preaching, that Jesus is — not a great teacher or wise man — but Lord. (Read Colossians 1 or Philippians 2, for example, both of which date from a couple of decades after the resurrection of Jesus.)

(The point of this section, incidentally, isn't to "prove" to you that Jesus is divine. It's to show you that early Christians worshiped him as Lord, not just followed him as a wise, mortal teacher. To figure out what you believe about Jesus, don't depend on me or, for heaven's sake, Dan Brown. Go meet Jesus yourself, not through a novel, but through the Gospels themselves.)

The understanding of Jesus' shared nature with God only deepened over the next few centuries, as a quick survey of any collection of writings from the period will show. Tatian, to take just one example, was a Christian writer who lived in the second century:

"We do not act as fools, O Greeks, nor utter idle tales, when we announce that God was born in the form of a man" (*Oration Against the Greeks*, p. 21).

During these centuries, as we've seen, Christian teachers were already having to clarify Christian belief in the face of heresy. One of the heresies that was a problem in the second century was called "Docetism," the name of which is derived from a Greek word meaning "I seem." Docetists believed that Jesus was divine *to the exclusion of any authentic humanity*. They believed that his human form and sufferings weren't real, but only a vision. The existence of Docetism shows, in an exaggerated way, that Jesus' divinity was certainly taken seriously before the fourth century.

This isn't the place to sort out all of the meanings and implications of Jesus' divine and human natures, but simply to point out how deeply wrong Brown's account of Christian thinking about Jesus is.

He claims that the notion of Jesus' divinity was invented by Constantine in the fourth century. As the witnesses of the New Testament and the first three hundred years of Christian thinking and worship make clear, it wasn't. And if we're really interested in what early Christians taught and believed, we're much better off actually going to a primary source than to a popular novel.

What's that source? The New Testament, of course, which anyone seriously interested in these matters should read, study, and reflect on.

And don't forget: In *The Da Vinci Code*, Brown doesn't once cite from any book of the New Testament as he discusses Jesus' identity. Not once.

Arius and the Council

Now, the Council of Nicaea *did* have something to do with the issue of Jesus' divinity, but not at all what *The Da Vinci Code* claims it did.

As you probably know, if you've tried to sort it out for even a minute or two, the reality of Jesus as fully human and fully divine is difficult to grasp and articulate, and raises all sorts of interesting and thorny questions, questions that are not explicitly and directly answered in Scripture.

The New Testament records what those who met Jesus experienced: a fully human man in whom they encountered God, who forgave sins as God did, spoke with God's authority, and could not be defeated by death. How to explain it? How to define it?

That took several centuries, and, as is so often the case, the need to more closely and clearly define Jesus' identity occurred in the context of conflict. Ideas would rise up — that Jesus wasn't actually really human, that God just took on the form of a human person like a costume (Docetism) — which were clearly inconsistent with the witness of the apostles. As a result, bishops and theologians would have to re-articulate the witness of the apostles in ways that made sense for their own times and answered the questions that people were asking them.

It wasn't easy, because this is, as we said, a supremely difficult concept for us to get our minds around. But remember what the bottom line was for those defending the ancient knowledge of Jesus as fully human and fully divine. It was: How can we talk about Jesus in a way that is completely faithful to the full, complex picture of him that we read in the apostolic witnesses? For Jesus *is* described as being hungry, frightened, and angry in the Gospels. He *is* described as acting with the authority of God and rising from the dead. Any way that we talk about Jesus must be faithful to the whole, mysterious, exhilarating witness recorded in the Gospels and in other early Christian writings.

In the early fourth century, a particularly attractive way out of the conundrum appeared on the scene, propagated by a presbyter (priest) named Arius, from Alexandria, in Egypt.

Arius taught that Jesus was not fully God. He was, certainly, the highest of God's creatures, but he did not completely share in God's identity and nature. His ideas proved to be very popular, very quickly, and it was *this* conflict — between the followers of Arius and the followers of traditional Christianity — that the Council of Nicaea was called to resolve.

They did so by reaffirming Jesus' divine nature, in philosophical terms, because that was the type of language in which Arius posed his argument. The result is what we read in the Nicene Creed, that Jesus is: "God from God, Light from Light, true God from true God, begotten, not made, one in Being with the Father...."

As Scripture scholar Luke Timothy Johnson puts it in his book *The Creed*:

"The bishops at the Council of Nicaea therefore considered themselves to be correcting a distortion, not inventing a new doctrine. They had to use the philosophical language of being because that had become the language of analysis, and because Scripture did not provide any terms precise enough to say what they thought needed to be said ... they considered themselves thereby not to be perverting but preserving the full testimony of Scripture" (p. 131).

And, yes, this discussion was confirmed by a vote, which Brown so breathlessly reports, and which is supposed to undercut the entire venture. Well, the truth is that in Jewish and Christian tradition, the affirmation of God's will and wisdom has been sought in many ways. We read, for example, of leaders being chosen by lot in both the Old and New Testament, because those choosing believed that God would guide the result.

And it wasn't, as Brown claims, even a close vote. Only two bishops out of about three hundred (the exact count varies) voted in support of Arius' diminished view of Jesus.

Wrong Again

So we see, once again, that just about everything Brown says about this aspect of Christian history is incorrect:

He says that up until the fourth century, "Christianity" was a movement formed around the idea of Jesus as a "mortal prophet." A simple reading of the New Testament, written a few decades after Jesus' resurrection, shows that this is not so. Early Christians preached Jesus as Lord.

He says that the Council of Nicaea invented the idea of the divinity of Christ. It did not. It acted to preserve the integrity of the ancient testimony to Jesus, mysteriously human and divine.

Wrong again, on every score.

Next?

For Further Reading

The Creed: What Christians Believe and Why It Matters, by Luke Timothy Johnson, Doubleday, 2003.

Lord Jesus Christ: Devotion to Jesus in Earliest Christianity, by Larry W. Hurtado, Wm. B. Eerdmans Publishing, 2003.

Questions for Review

1. What are some passages from Scripture that reveal what the first Christians believed about Jesus?
2. What was the problem addressed by the Council of Nicaea?

Questions for Discussion

1. What was at stake in the Arian controversy?
2. What do you think about Constantine's role in religious matters?

four

TOPPLED KINGS?

Let's pause for a moment and take stock.

So far, in our journey through the historical vision so blithely asserted in *The Da Vinci Code*, we've found that:

- The sources for these assertions about the earliest Christian history range from the completely fantastic and baseless to irrelevant.
- Brown, in constructing his version of events, uses not one source of the period in question — not the New Testament, the writings of bishops and teachers, liturgical documents, or histories.
- His presentations of the formation of the Scriptural Canon, the Council of Nicaea, Constantine's reign, and the early Christian understanding of Jesus' identity are all completely, without exception, wrong, with no relationship to any past or present understanding of these events.

There really seems no point in going on, does there? But, of course, we're not even close to being finished with the misstatements and historical falsehoods in this book, so — onward.

Did Jesus really "topple kings," anyway?

Toppling Kings and Inspiring Millions

It's time to explore what *The Da Vinci Code* purports to be the real story behind Jesus' ministry. What did he teach? What was he trying to accomplish?

One would think, naturally, that the first place we'd look when trying to answer this not-particularly-knotty question would be the Gospels found in the New Testament. After all, they all date from only decades after Jesus' death, and although they each emphasize different aspects of Jesus' ministry and identity, they are also in substantial agreement about the general focus of Jesus' teaching and the pattern of his life.

One would think — but no.

In presenting Jesus, Brown can't be bothered with the Gospels.

Teabing tells Sophie that Jesus, of course, was a real person who, as the prophesied Messiah, "toppled kings, inspired millions, and founded new philosophies. . . . Understandably, his life was recorded by thousands of followers across the land" (p. 231).

Well, no.

We know a little bit about the history of Palestine and the Roman Empire during Jesus' life. There is no record of a Jewish layman from Nazareth toppling any of them.

It's hard to estimate such things, but we can safely guess that the population of the areas where Jesus is said to have preached — in Galilee to the north and Samaria and Judea to the south — had, according to the highest estimate, about half a million people, most of whom probably never heard Jesus preach.

That's a long way from "millions."

Why is Teabing saying this? What is it based on? Nothing in the historical record, that's for sure.

Indeed, the Gospels paint a far more complex picture of Jesus' public ministry. Certainly, he was sometimes met by huge crowds, huge enough that once he had to push a boat out on a lake to preach to them. But he was also rejected, not only by some religious leaders, but also by the people of his hometown (see Luke 4:29-30), and other whole villages as well (see Matthew 8:34). His disciples followed and listened to him, but also squabbled among themselves, and fled when the going got tough.

Brown describes Jesus as if he were some kind of first-century rock star, followed by adoring crowds, continually blown away by his presence.

Not so.

What Was He Talking About?

In *The Da Vinci Code*, Brown never really comes out and directly states what Jesus' message was. He makes frequent allusions to Jesus being revered as a teacher and a prophet, but doesn't get more specific than that.

The implication though, is that Jesus' real message is centered on those Gnostic writings we discussed before, and this whole business of the "sacred feminine."

That, after all, is the point of the book: that the ancient reverence for the "sacred feminine" had been lost, and that somehow Jesus, especially in his relationship with Mary Magdalene, intended to restore it and, through her, make sure that the world got back on track.

Where does this come from? Perhaps from Brown's reading of Gnostic-Christian writings, which do imply an original androgynous state for humanity that should be restored.

We've laid out the problem with that before, of course. The Gnostic-Christian writings are in no way traceable to any early witnesses to Jesus. Any allusions they contain to known sayings of Jesus are dependent on older documents — the Synoptic Gospels (Matthew, Mark, and Luke) most of the time.

The second problem, if that doesn't convince you, is that Brown's use of the Gnostic documents is highly selective. Gnostic texts that have come down to us are a diverse lot, because, of course, Gnosticism was diverse. But, beside occasional echoes of the "sacred feminine," you will more frequently find abstruse, esoteric systems of thought involving sparks, passwords, good and evil forces, and myriad levels of heaven. You will also find anti-Judaism and, inconveniently, some misogyny, as well.

Proponents of the value of Gnostic texts in retrieving some kind of lost Jesus movement that valued this thing we call the "sacred feminine," never seem to mention other passages, as noted by Philip Jenkins in his book *The Hidden Gospels:*

"The Gnostic Jesus had come to provide spiritual liberation, and repeatedly in the texts, we find variants on the theme that the Savior had come 'to destroy the works of the female.' In *The Dialogue of the Savior*, we read, typically that 'Judas said, ... "When we pray, how should we pray?" The Lord said, "Pray in the place where there is no woman." '... It is bizarre to denounce Christianity for celibacy and hatred of the body, while ignoring exactly the same flaws in Gnosticism ..." (pp. 211-212).

So, no, there's no evidence that Jesus toppled kings, founded philosophies or embraced the "sacred feminine." The early witnesses, however, are not silent about what he did say, and what they relate is consistent both across the Scriptures and in the prayer life — the point of contact between Christians and the living Lord — of the early Christian communities.

The focus of Jesus' teaching was the kingdom, or reign of God. He articulated this message in preaching, parables, and in his relationships with other people. He indicated through his words and actions that God was love — love, compassion, and mercy for all people. This love of God was, his words and actions revealed, pres-

---

"Simon Peter said to them, 'Let Mary leave us, for women are not worthy of Life.' Jesus said, 'I myself shall lead her in order to make her male, so that she too may become a living spirit resembling you males. For every woman who will make herself male will enter the Kingdom of Heaven' " (*Gospel of Thomas*, p. 114 [*The Nag Hammadi Library*, James M. Robinson, editor. Harper and Row, 1976., p. 130]).

This is the final passage from the best-known Gnostic writing, a passage that is not quoted in *The Da Vinci Code*.

ent in him. Where Jesus acted, the kingdom was present. We are a part of God's kingdom when we live in union with Jesus and pattern our lives after his: a pattern of loving, sacrificial discipleship that does not count the cost.

This focus is no secret, by the way. Reading the New Testament reveals an amazing consistency in this general picture of what Jesus was all about: God-centered discipleship, love, sacrifice, and joy.

A More Human Jesus

One of the points frequently made in *The Da Vinci Code* is that traditional Christianity was determined to suppress the Gnostic writings that make reference to him because they present a more "human" picture of Jesus, which is the one that had dominated for centuries before Constantine came on the scene. And so on.

We've been through this in the last chapter, pointing out the understanding of Jesus as Lord, as divine, as the Son of God, that it is clear in New Testament writings, which date from the first century.

But it's important to dig just a little bit more into this claim that the official story emphasized Jesus as divine at the expense of his humanity, which the Gnostic writings bring out. Brown says this a few times, but never gives any specific evidence to support his characterization. Should we believe him?

Perhaps not. Anyone who takes as little as an hour to peruse one of the canonical Gospels alongside a couple of these Gnostic accounts, can see how false this characterization is.

For when you read the Gnostic writings, you might be surprised that you don't find a particularly "human" Jesus. He is a teacher, but there is little about him that is recognizably or uniquely human. He shares wisdom, reveals secrets, and wanders around in a gently spiritual fog, and talks, and talks. And talks.

This makes sense, of course, since Gnostic systems of thinking generally devalued the material world, including the human body. Gnostic writings about Jesus pointedly ignore, for example, the Passion and death of Jesus. So sure, read over the favorite Gnostic texts, such as the *Gospel of Philip*, the *Gospel of Thomas* and the maybe-Gnostic *Gospel of Mary*. Read all of those long dialogues. Then crack open, say, the Book of Matthew to chapter 26: 37-38:

"And taking with him Peter and the two sons of Zebedee, he began to be sorrowful and troubled. Then he said to them, 'My soul is very sorrowful, even to death; remain here, and watch with me.' "

And then peruse the rest of the gospels. You will read of Jesus eating, drinking, being angry, frightened, lonely and grieving, suffering and dying.

Only someone who is totally unfamiliar with the Gospels could hold that they present an "inhuman" portrait of Jesus. In fact, it's the opposite. The reason Christian teachers fought so hard against Gnostic and similar ideas was precisely because those systems *deemphasized* Jesus' humanity, and were, as such, unfaithful to the ancient witness preserved in the New Testament.

But perhaps, when Brown and others like him suggest that we need a more "human" Jesus, who's supposedly not presented to us in the Gospels, they're not concerned with the qualities we've discussed above. They just might be talking about something else. They just might be talking about sex.

Was Jesus Married?

In the next chapter, we're going to explore the wonderful, intriguing character of Mary Magdalene (who is, incidentally, honored as a saint in Catholicism and Orthodoxy, not reviled, as Brown suggests), and the evidence regarding Jesus' relationship to her, specifically.

As long as we're talking about the general contours and direction of Jesus' life, as *The Da Vinci Code* presents it, this is a good place to talk about the question of Jesus' marriage in general.

It's important to state right from the beginning that any doubts about Jesus being married aren't offered out of "fear" or a hatred of sexuality. That's quite often what proponents of a married Jesus will suggest — that gosh, we can't handle a married Jesus because we're so weird about sex, and it would just shatter our faith to even think about it because we hate sex.

Oh, really?

Fear or denial is not the issue here. The issue is what the texts and the best evidence reveal, when viewed honestly and objectively.

In *The Da Vinci Code*, our friend Teabing (of course) lets Sophie know that, sure, Jesus was married, saying, point blank, "It's a matter of historical record" (p. 244).

Where?

As we've pointed out, the best "historical records" we have to reveal the life of Jesus are the canonical Gospels, which were written just decades after his death and resurrection. They have their limits, certainly, as do all ancient documents, but when we want to answer questions about what Jesus did and what he was like, those texts would be the place to start (texts that, we will repeat tirelessly, Brown never references).

And the big news is   they don't mention Jesus being married. Ever.

Now, there's an argument related to this silence, and someone even wrote an entire book based on this argument, and we've heard it many times: The Gospels are silent about Jesus' marriage because being married was the normal state of a Jewish man of the period, so it was taken for granted, and not deemed important enough to mention.

Brown suggests that silence works the other way, too. If he weren't married, Gospel writers would have taken a minute or two to explain or defend it because it would have been so unusual.

Of course, an argument from silence is a tricky argument, but there's more to say about the matter than just letting it rest there. John Meier of The Catholic University of America has very ably unpacked the evidence in his book *A Marginal Jew*. We'll consider two of his points here.

First, Meier critiques the argument from silence because the Gospels are not at all silent about Jesus' other relationships. They mention his parents and his other relatives with great frequency. They describe him coming into contact, and even conflict, with people from Nazareth, his hometown. Luke even names the women who were among Jesus' disciples and followed him, ministering to him: Mary Magdalene, Joanna, and Susanna (see Luke 8:2, 3).

Given this definite non-silence about Jesus' family ties and about the women who followed him, there's no reason for a wife to go unmentioned.

Next, Meier addresses the claim that marriage was absolutely normative for Jewish men, especially rabbis, of Jesus' time, and an unmarried Jesus would require special defending in order to preserve his credibility. There was no way Jesus would be taken seriously if he were unmarried.

This assumption is simply not true. Meier faults this claim on several levels. First, Jesus was not a rabbi. He was called "rabbi," which means "teacher," by his disciples, but the evidence doesn't suggest that he was, in any formal, institutional sense, a rabbi.

The claim also is faulty because it presents a monolithic portrait of first-century Judaism, which does not reflect reality. There was, in fact, at least one Jewish sect of the period whose members practiced celibacy: the Essenes, who lived in community at Qumran, near the Dead Sea, and who left the Dead Sea Scrolls.

There is also definitely a tradition in Judaism of figures whose lives were so wholly given to God's work and the Law that they were celibate. The prophet Jeremiah is one. Jewish traditions that elaborated on the scriptural texts offered a portrait of Moses who, once he encountered God on Mt. Sinai, was celibate. John the Baptist, also most certainly an historical figure, was unmarried, as was, most scholars believe, Paul.

Meier concludes:

"When we correlate all these tendencies, we notice that the first century A.D. was populated by some striking celibate individuals and groups: some Essenes and Qumranites, the Therapeutae, John the Baptist, Jesus, Paul, Epictetus, Apollinius, and various wandering Cynics. Celibacy was always a rare and sometimes offensive choice in the first century A.D. But it was a viable choice" (p. 342).

So there you have it: There's no evidence from the most reliable texts that Jesus was married, and knowledge of the milieu of the first century suggests that it wouldn't be absolutely unheard of for an individual single-mindedly devoted to God to be unmarried.

Truth and Consequences

The *Da Vinci Code* claim that traditional Christianity devalues Jesus' humanity is just bogus. The Gospels consistently present us with a real, very human figure, as opposed to the rather ethereal figure we find in Gnostic writings. Many of the theological struggles and conflicts of the first four centuries of Christian history reflect the determination of Christian teachers to be faithful to the Gospel record and, as mysterious as it may be, stand firm behind the full humanity of Jesus.

We might also take a look, for just a moment, at Christian devotion and art through the centuries, since that supposedly fateful day in A.D. 325 when Constantine pushed Jesus' humanity out of the picture.

Christian prayer through the ages has often connected with Jesus through his "sorrows," through his compassion, and through his suffering. Christian-inspired art presents us with an infant Jesus suckling at his mother's breast, a man bleeding and beaten, and even a silent corpse, returned to his mother's arms.

The idea that anyone could take seriously *The Da Vinci Code* scenario tells us a lot. It tells us that too many people — both inside and outside Christianity — are totally disconnected from the Gospel portrait of Jesus and the rich tradition of Christian theological and spiritual reflection on the mystery of Jesus' humanity. Whatever they are learning about Jesus, they are not learning it from the Gospels and Christian tradition, which then leaves them open to distortions such as we find in *The Da Vinci Code*.

Christianity doesn't value the humanity of Jesus? The truth is as close as the image that's hanging on the wall of the church down the street. Two beams. A man. Not a ghost. Not a myth. A man.

For Further Reading

The Real Jesus, by Luke Timothy Johnson, Harper San Francisco, 1996.

Questions for Review

1. Why is it false to say that the Gnostic writings present a "more human" vision of Jesus than the canonical Gospels do?
2. What evidence points to the likelihood of Jesus being unmarried?

Questions for Discussion

1. What were some of the varied reactions to Jesus during his ministry? Why do you think people responded to him in different ways?
2. Why is Jesus' full humanity so important in Christian belief?

five

MARY, CALLED MAGDALENE

The Da Vinci Code isn't just about Jesus, of course. It's also very much about that purported wife, Mary Magdalene.

Before we get to what we know about Mary Magdalene (which isn't much), let's do a quick run-through of what Brown says.

According to Brown, she was a Jewish woman from the tribe of Benjamin, who was married to Jesus and bore his child. Jesus intended his church to be in her hands, that church being about the reintegration of the "sacred feminine" into human life and consciousness. She escaped to the Jewish community in Provence after Jesus' crucifixion, where she and her daughter, Sarah, were protected. Her womb is the "Holy Grail." Her bones are under the glass pyramidal entrance to the Louvre. The Priory of Sion and the Knights Templar were dedicated to protecting her story and her relics. The Priory worships her "as the Goddess... and the Divine Mother" (p. 255).

Jewish royalty... Jesus' wife... Holy Grail... Goddess.

That's quite a résumé.

Considering that Mary of Magdala is mentioned just a few times in the Gospels, where could all of these ideas come from?

Well, the answer to that is right in the novel, as Teabing, our noted scholar, shows off his library, saying, "The royal bloodline has been chronicled in exhaustive detail by scores of historians." (There we go with that patina of scholarship again.)

He cites *The Templar Revelation* and *Holy Blood, Holy Grail* — two works of schlock pseudo-history and conspiracy theory, and *The Goddess in the Gospels* and *The Woman With the Alabaster Jar*, both by Margaret Starbird, who, among other points, uses numerology — the sum of the numbers in the name she was called — to conclude that Mary Magdalene was revered as a goddess among early Christians:

"They understood the 'numbers theology' of the Hellenistic world, numbers coded in the New Testament that were based on the ancient canon of sacred geometry derived by the Pythagoreans centuries before. . . . It was no accident that the epithet of Mary Magdalene bore the numbers that to the educated of the time identified her as the 'Goddess in the Gospels' " (*Mary Magdalene: The Beloved*, by Margaret Starbird; www.magdalene.org/beloved-essay.htm).

Well, we really have to stop and think about this for a moment. The Gospels can't be consulted or read at face value, and not for a second are we allowed to believe that they communicate any truth about the events they describe. But, do they communicate in code that early Christians viewed Mary Magdalene as a goddess?

Well, if they viewed her as a goddess, why didn't they just come out and say it? Why bother with all of this Jesus-crucified-risen stuff when you can just worship the Magdalene, if that's what you really wanted to do? It's not as if there were any social, cultural, or political censure directed at those who wanted to worship a goddess. It sure wouldn't get you arrested, imprisoned, and executed, as would a faith centered on a certain other figure, who shall remain nameless and who supposedly wasn't worshiped until the fourth century.

So once again, before we get too excited about the historical assertions in *The Da Vinci Code*, we're reminded of the importance of checking sources. In terms of the Mary Magdalene material, these are the basics:

Mary Magdalene as Jesus' wife, mother of his child, and the real "Holy Grail": *Holy Blood, Holy Grail* and *The Templar Revelation*;

Mary Magdalene as a goddess, as the source of the "sacred feminine": Margaret Starbird's work;

Mary Magdalene as the designated leader of early Christianity: a variety of contemporary scholars working with Gnostic texts.

Before we go into any more detail on any of these points, it's good to stop, forget the speculation, and go back to the place where we first hear of Mary Magdalene: the Gospels.

Who Was Mary Magdalene?

There is no doubt that Mary was an historical figure. She is mentioned by name in the Gospels and plays an extremely important role, along with other women, in relation to the Passion and resurrection of Jesus.

Only one Gospel mentions her outside of those last days of Jesus. It's Luke, who writes of Jesus' ministry of preaching and proclaiming the Good News, accompanied by the Twelve Apostles, and:

"... and also some women who had been healed of evil spirits and infirmities: Mary, called Magdalene, from whom seven demons had gone out, and Joanna, the wife of Chuza, Herod's steward, and Susanna, and many others, who provided for them out of their means" (8:2, 3).

These women from Galilee, it seems, chose to cast their lot in with Jesus, giving support through practical help, such as providing meals and perhaps even money.

For other unequivocal Mary sightings, we must move to the end of the Gospels, where in every one of them she is described standing in witness to the crucifixion and burial of Jesus, then coming to the tomb on Easter morning to anoint his body.

"Magdalene" is not Mary's last name — people in these times did not have last names. They were identified by their relationship to their father or by their hometown. Most scholars believe that Magdalene means "of Magdala," a town on the western shore of the Sea of Galilee.

It is there, according to all four Gospels, that Mary receives the Good News, first from an angel (see Matthew 28:1-7; Mark 16:1-8; Luke 24:1-10), and then from Jesus himself (see Matthew 28:9-10; John 20:16-18), who not only appears to Mary and the others and tells them not to be afraid, but instructs them to go and tell the apostles the Good News.

So Mary Magdalene was, indeed, one of the first evangelizers, or, as Eastern Christianity has long called her, the "equal-to-the-apostles," as she announced the Good News that Jesus had risen.

Then What Happened?

Notice what was missing (besides the goddess business, naturally) from our look at the few times Mary Magdalene is mentioned: Wasn't she a repentant prostitute?

This is a big deal in *The Da Vinci Code*, which often refers to Mary's identification as a prostitute as part of a vicious Church plot hatched to counter any suspicion, or even (it's said) historical evidence, of Mary Magdalene's leadership in early Christianity.

Two points: First, this association of Mary Magdalene with prostitution did indeed evolve over the centuries in Western Christianity (although not in the East). However, there's no evidence that it was done, as Brown and his sources assert, out of malice, misogyny, or a fear of female authority.

There are several Marys mentioned in the Gospels, and a few other significant, although unnamed, women, as well. Readers of Scripture have long either confused the Marys, or wondered if there might be a reason to associate a Mary mentioned in one place with a Mary or other woman mentioned elsewhere.

There are, for example, two different stories of women anointing Jesus' feet with their hair. In Luke 7:36-50, Jesus encounters a "woman . . . who was a sinner," who, weeping in repentance, anoints and bathes his feet, then dries them with her hair. Her anointing is in gratitude for forgiveness of her sins (which, we might add, are not explicitly identified). In John 12:1-8, Jesus, on his way to

Jerusalem, stops at the home of Lazarus (raised from the dead in John 11) and his sisters, Martha and Mary. Mary anoints his feet and dries them with her hair as a solemn prefiguring of the anointing he will receive at his burial, just a few days away.

The story of the penitent woman in Luke appears just verses before he mentions Mary Magdalene by name, so some, including most significantly Pope Gregory I in a sermon in A.D. 591, associate the two. The trouble with this theory is that when he introduces a person with a name, Luke names him or her specifically. If this woman was indeed Mary Magdalene, many believe, he would have identified her right away instead of the second time he mentions her.

Then, because Mary of Bethany anoints Jesus before he enters Jerusalem, some traditions connected her with that anointing woman in Luke 7, and then with the named Mary Magdalene in Luke 8, conflating all three women into one.

This is exactly what happened in the Western Church, which, from the early Middle Ages up until the liturgical calendar was reformed in 1969, used the feast day of Mary Magdalene on July 22 to remember all three women from each of those Gospel stories.

The Eastern Orthodox Church did not conflate these figures, however, always treating them as separate people. The Orthodox Church gives great honor to Mary Magdalene, calling her "myrrh-bearer" (one of the spices used in anointing) and "equal-to-the-apostles."

Now, here's an extremely important, vital point:

Brown suggests, repeatedly, that Mary Magdalene was marginalized and demonized by traditional Christianity, which painted her, he says, as a wanton woman, a prostitute, and so on, supposedly in an effort to diminish her importance.

Like so much of what we find in Brown, this is not only wrong — it simply makes no sense.

Christianity, both East and West, has honored Mary Magdalene as a saint.

A saint. They've named churches after her, prayed at her pur-ported tombs before what was believed to be her relics, and ascribed miracles to her.

How in the world, in what universe, is that demonizing?

Answer: It's not.

As for that prostitution theme, even in those parts of Chris-tianity that did link Mary Magdalene with the "woman . . . who was a sinner" of Luke 7, her sin was not emphasized because, of course, Christianity is not about dwelling on sin after repentance. That's the point of faith in Jesus. No, Mary Magdalene, as the leg-ends about her attest, was remembered primarily in her role as a witness to the risen Jesus.

Before the Renaissance, Mary Magdalene imagery was rather sedate. It was only with the Renaissance that we encounter the disheveled, half-clothed, loose-haired repentant Magdalene. Renaissance artists had a growing interest in a more naturalistic presentation of the human form, and the more explicit integration of human emotion into artistic representation. Mary Magdalene's presentation had far less to do with how the Christian Church was speaking of her than with artistic interests.

"Magdalene Christianity"

This is the phrase that scholar Jane Schaberg uses to describe her vision of the future possibilities of Christianity, based on her hypotheses about the past.

Schaberg and other contemporary feminist scholars, such as Karen King of Harvard Divinity School, have used the prominent role of Mary Magdalene in a few of the Gnostic writings of the late second century onward to suggest that they reveal a power struggle within Christianity, between a party of Peter and that of Mary Magdalene.

In *The Da Vinci Code*, Teabing declares as much, declaring that Leonardo da Vinci's art gives clues to this truth as well, a truth that he notes is contained in "these unaltered gospels."

Mary Magdalene in Provence: Part of Brown's story of Mary Magdalene claims that she ended up in Provence, in southern France. Legends in Catholic tradition do place Mary there, and give credit to her for evangelizing the people of the area. Eastern Christian traditions claim that she went to Ephesus and evangelized there with St. John.

Let us quickly run down the logical problems with this as it's articulated in the novel:

If Peter's party — which we can assume is the "winner" Brown is always talking about who writes history — really was so adamant to purge Mary and diminish her importance, why would they retain her prime role in the Resurrection accounts as the first person to receive the Good News?

Brown has told us before that before Constantine did his evil deed in A.D. 325, Christians everywhere simply believed in Jesus as a "mortal man." If that was the case, who, exactly, were the Peter party? Presumably they were the "winners," which means they must have believed in Jesus' divinity, because that's the view that "won," but then wasn't Jesus' divinity invented in A.D. 325? So where were they that whole time?

Finally, moving away from the pure pleasure of unpacking these howling logical inconsistencies, we want to turn to the evidence.

Is there evidence of an orthodox Christian element in a battle for supremacy with a Magdalene party, and demeaning her in the process?

No. It's pure speculation, based on ideologically motivated reading of texts dating from at least a hundred years after Jesus' life. Some Gnostic-Christian sects that evolved in the late second century did, obviously, grant Mary Magdalene a prime role. The passages in the Gnostic writings that suggest intimacy between Jesus and Mary do not have any elements traceable to the first century, and serve a theological point, usually to give support to their version of Christianity and diminish the role of Peter and the apostles.

But here's the thing. If orthodox Christian writers of the period knew this, and if it concerned them, they probably would have addressed it directly, for they did, indeed, speak negatively of some Gnostic sects in which women acted as leaders or prophets. However, the texts we have don't specifically critique any group for viewing Mary as a leader at Peter's expense. Further, oddly enough, during this period, the period in which Mary was supposed to have been demonized by the orthodox, we read nothing but praise for her.

Hippolytus, writing in Rome in the late second and early third centuries, describes Mary Magdalene as a New Eve, whose faithfulness stands in contrast to the sin of Eve in the Garden (an image often used for Mary, the Mother of Jesus, as well). He also calls Mary Magdalene "the apostle to the apostles." St. Ambrose and St. Augustine, both writing a century or so later, also spoke of Mary Magdalene as the New Eve.

So once again, nothing Brown suggests makes sense. During the period Mary's party is supposedly battling Peter's party for the soul of the Church, Church fathers are writing high praise of her and treasuring Gospels that feature her role in the Resurrection appearances.

There is nothing in the reality of Mary Magdalene in Scripture, or in the way that she has been treated in Eastern or Western Christian tradition, that supports anything Brown contends.

As we keep finding, though, the truth is much more interesting, and authentically inspiring, than anything the fantasies in *The Da Vinci Code* might suggest.

For Further Reading

Women in the New Testament, by Mary Ann Getty-Sullivan, Liturgical Press, 2001.

Questions for Review

1. According to the Gospels, who was Mary Magdalene?
2. How has Mary Magdalene been remembered through Christian history?

Questions for Discussion

1. What can contemporary Christians learn from Mary Magdalene's prominence in the accounts of the Resurrection?
2. What role do women seem to play in Jesus' ministry? What does their witness communicate about Christian discipleship?

six

THE AGE OF THE GODDESS?

O ne of the most appealing elements of *The Da Vinci Code* to many readers is the idea of the "sacred feminine."

They are intrigued by what author Brown purports to reveal to them about the past: that there was a period of time deep in history during which, at the very least, humanity lived conscious of the need to keep the male and female elements of life in balance, and did so through the worship of both male and female deities and spirits. Even more intriguing is the possibility that there was, as Langdon tells Sophie, a period in which "matriarchal paganism" ruled the world.

Readers are also interested in Brown's claims about women and Christianity: that Jesus taught the reunion of the feminine and masculine aspects of reality, and that women were leaders in early Christianity, until "patriarchal Christianity" waged "a campaign of propaganda that demonized the "sacred feminine," obliterating the goddess from modern religion forever" (p. 124).

It's easy to see the appeal of such a vision of the past, especially for women who feel disengaged from Christianity for what they understand (rightly or wrongly) to be its unjust conceptualization and treatment of women.

So, sure, one can see how a vision is attractive. But what use is any vision, what real source of strength or inspiration can it be, if it's not true?

The "Sacred Feminine"

Brown draws on a couple of strands of thinking when he writes (as he does, incessantly) of the "sacred feminine."

First, he's appealing to a school of thought that emerged in the nineteenth century, which posited that ancient people's worship of goddesses had sprung from a more elemental worship of a great "Mother Goddess," explained in part by the great reverence ancient people had for the mystery and power of childbirth. Archaeological finds of pregnant female figures, among other artifacts, were used to support this theory, which evolved in the late 20th century to declare, as writer Charlotte Allen puts it, that:

"This nature-attuned, woman-respecting, peaceful, and egalitarian culture prevailed in what is now Western Europe for thousands of years… until Indo-European invaders swept across the region, introducing warrior gods, weapons designed for killing human beings, and patriarchal civilization" (*The Atlantic*, January 2001).

In recent years, however, the ideology driving these conclusions, the ambiguous nature of these purported artifacts, and the discovery of weapons and clear evidence of traditional gender-based division of labor in many of these sites, has driven a stake into the myth of the Mother Goddess. There is no evidence to suggest that such an era ever existed.

One of Brown's more bizarre contentions is that even ancient Judaism valued the "sacred feminine" as a distinct aspect of the divine, evidenced by their practice of having ritualistic sex in the Temple in Jerusalem.

This is quite strange, and it's difficult to say where Brown gets this from. There is certainly no evidence whatsoever to support it, and it even stands in direct opposition to what the Hebrew Scriptures indicate is required for those involved in Temple sacrifice and worship: scrupulous ritual purity, which involved abstention from sexual activity for a period before involvement in worship. Jesuit Scripture scholar Gerald O'Collins neatly eviscerates this assertion:

"Apropos of Judaism, Brown introduces some stunning errors about ritualistic sex and God. Old Testament scholars agree that prostitution was sometimes used to obtain money for the temple.

But there is no convincing evidence for sacred or ritual prostitution, and none at all for Israelite men coming to the temple to experience the divine and achieve spiritual wholeness by having sex with priestesses (p. 309). On the same page, Brown explains that the Holy of Holies 'housed not only God but also His powerful female equal, Shekinah.' A word not found as such in the Bible but in later rabbinic writings, *Shekinah* refers to the nearness of God to his people and not to some female consort" (*America*, December 15, 2003).

O'Collins also eviscerates Brown's claim in the same passage that YHWH is derived from Jehovah, which is, of course, the complete opposite of reality:

"It is also breathtaking nonsense to assert as a 'fact' that the sacred tetragrammaton, YHWH, was "derived from Jehovah, an androgynous physical union between the masculine *Jah* and the pre-Hebraic name for Eve, *Havah*." YHWH is written in Hebrew without any vowel signs. Jews did not pronounce the sacred name, but "Yahweh" was apparently the correct vocalization of the four consonants. In the sixteenth century, some Christian writers introduced Jehovah under the mistaken notion that the vowels they used were the correct ones. Jehovah is an artificial name created less than five hundred years ago, and certainly not an ancient, androgynous name from which YHWH derived" (ibid).

Ancient cultures did, of course, worship female deities, as do animist and polytheistic systems (such as Hinduism) today. Most of the female deities are consorts of male deities. Ancient systems do reflect an awareness of male and female principles in the weave of reality, but they do not reveal any particular consciousness or reverence for the "sacred feminine," as Brown consistently describes it.

A close look at Catholic and Orthodox Christianity, as it's been practiced over two thousand years, doesn't exactly reveal a spirituality drenched in patriarchal imagery at the expense of the feminine. But more on that later.

Finally, one would expect that societies nourished by the type of spiritual system Brown suggests would be profoundly egalitarian. Surprisingly, we find no examples of such egalitarianism in any ancient culture that worshiped both gods and goddesses, or even those that practiced ritual sex (not nearly as universal as he suggests), which was, in Brown's view, supposed to join the masculine and feminine principles in an ecstatic, life-giving whole.

Heretics and Witches

After the matriarchal age had been supplanted, the dedication to the feminine must, according to the next step in this scenario, go underground.

In terms of Christianity, Brown, using the work of various contemporary writers on women and early Christianity, suggests that there was a branch of the Jesus movement that was woman-centered. In Brown's scenario, this is what we see when we read the Gnostic writings that put Mary Magdalene at front and center.

These were, however, systems far removed from the mainstream of Christianity. They used the figure of Christ and some of his teachings as a means for expressing essentially Gnostic ideas. They had no direct ties to early Christian witness, nor, on the other hand, were they elements in a continuous ancient tradition centered on the "sacred feminine."

In *The Da Vinci Code*, they are. After orthodox Christianity "won" at Nicaea, the story continues, it continued to suppress evidence of pagan (which equals devotion to the "sacred feminine") belief, or co-opt them. It also viciously destroyed those who persisted in the old ways, particularly as witches.

Five million, to be specific.

Yes, you heard that right. Brown states that this hostility to women, bubbling for centuries, finally came to the surface as the Catholic Church executed five million women during three hundred years of witch hunts. (Brown doesn't specify which centuries, but we can assume he means 1500-1800, the years commonly studied as a period of more intense witch-hunting in Europe.)

You might have heard this before — it's a figure that you often encounter on Internet discussions of the evils of the Catholic Church. But, like so much in this book, it's wrong.

Charlotte Allen, in her *Atlantic* magazine article, summarizes the most recent research into the subject (which is considerable), saying that most scholars have settled on around forty thousand witchcraft-related executions during this period, some by Catholic bodies, others by Protestant bodies, and most by governments. About twenty percent of recorded witchcraft charges were made, incidentally, against men.

"The most thorough recent study of historical witchcraft is *Witches and Neighbors* (1996) by Robin Briggs, a historian at Oxford University. Briggs pored over the documents of European witch trials and concluded that most of them took place during a relatively short period, 1550-1630, and were largely confined to parts of present-day France, Switzerland, and Germany that were already racked by the religious and political turmoil of the Reformation. The accused witches, far from including a large number of independent-minded women, were mostly poor and unpopular. Their accusers were typically ordinary citizens (often other women), not clerical or secular authorities. In fact, the authorities generally disliked trying witchcraft cases and acquitted more than half of all defendants. Briggs also discovered that none of the accused witches who were found guilty and put to death had been charged specifically with practicing a pagan religion" (Allen, "The Scholar and the Goddess," *Atlantic Monthly*, January 2001).

It is, of course, tragic and in our eyes unjust, that any men or women were executed for any of these reasons by anyone. For most of human history, however, most societies have not protected freedom of thought, religion, or expression. In fact, the exact opposite is the case. Most societies have placed serious restrictions on what members may say in public and what they may encourage others to

Is *Malleus Maleficarum* ("The Hammer of Witches") a real document? Yes, and while important, it was not the universal hand-
book for trying witches that Brown claims. It was written by a
Dominican, Heinrich Kramer, who claimed to have based it on
his experience of trying over a hundred cases. In fact, records
indicate he tried only eight women and was expelled by the
bishop of the next town he attempted to work in.

do, and they have often backed up that conviction with harsh pun-
ishment for offenders. This is not anything the Catholic or Protestant Churches invented. That, of course, doesn't make it any less
unfortunate that, in these periods of history, Christian churches were
not stronger witnesses to the Gospel.

Aren't We Forgetting Someone?

In *The Da Vinci Code*, Brown insists that over the past two thousand years, Christianity has been virulently patriarchal, anti-
woman, and determined to stamp out any hints of the "sacred
feminine" wherever they might arise.

Apparently, Brown has never heard of Mary, the Mother of
Jesus.

If you really want to understand how distant this novel's assertions are from the truth about Christianity, reflect for a moment
on that glaring, bizarre omission. And wonder why.
One can only conclude that paying any heed to the tremendous
import of Mary in Christian thought and expression would completely undermine Brown's contention that orthodox Christianity
lives in mortal fear of the "sacred feminine," so he naturally thought
it best to pretend it never happened.

But it did happen. As scholar Jaroslav Pelikan writes:

"... if we could enable the silent millions among Medieval women to recover their voices, the evidence that we do have from those relatively few who did leave a written record strongly suggests that it was with the figure of Mary that many of them identified themselves — with her humility, yes, but also with her defiance and with her victory.... Because of that role that she has been playing for the history of the past twenty centuries, the Virgin Mary has been the subject of more thought and discussion about what it means to be a woman than any other woman in Western history" (*Mary Through the Centuries*, p. 219).

When human beings attempt to understand and relate to God, the same humanity that makes intimacy with God possible, because humans are made in his image, also limits them. Our language can only say so much, our thinking about God can only go as far as our existence as embodied creatures of space, time, and particular experience in the world can take us.

But it is within that same world, using the stuff He has created, that God graciously meets us and makes himself known.

Teabing says that images of the goddess Isis nursing Horus were a "blueprint" for images of Mary and Jesus. Well, when it comes to mothers and children, there are obviously a few typical poses that would be common to any iconography, as is the case here. But Teabing implies a causal connection: Honoring Mary is in imitation of Isis-worship. No. In the Roman world, Isis was strongly associated with promiscuity, and the "miraculous" conception Teabing alludes to happened either by Isis reconstructing the body parts of her dead husband or by magic. The two have little in common (see *The Cult of the Virgin Mary*, Michael P. Carroll, Princeton University Press, 1986, pp. 8-9).

What Christians throughout history have experienced is that while Mary is not God, because she is the Mother of God, through her role in our salvation — saying "yes" to God, her *fiat* — her life reveals to us God's faithfulness, his compassion, and, yes, the fullness of his love, as it is revealed through the love of a mother.

The figure of Mary, the Mother of Jesus, is not unambiguous, and is multifaceted. Some Christians are even uncomfortable with attention to Mary, feeling that it crosses over into an area of expression and devotion that should be reserved for God alone. Which, of course, is as much an argument against Brown's assertions about Christian tradition as we need.

No matter what you think about Mary or about devotion to her, one thing that any of us with eyes to see can agree on is that she has played a vital, almost central role in Christian thinking, prayer, and devotion for hundreds of years.

Brown is wrong here, again. Christianity hasn't repressed attention to the "sacred feminine." In Mary, Catholic and Orthodox Christianity has, in fact, celebrated and nourished it. Some would even say too much.

Too ignore that is to ignore the truth. If truth matters, that is.

For Further Reading

Goddess Unmasked: The Rise of Neopagan Feminist Spirituality, by Philip Davis, Spence Publishers, 1998.

Mary Through the Ages: Her Place in the History of Culture, by Jaroslav Pelikan, Yale University Press, 1996.

Questions for Review

1. What is the evidence against the theory that the world once lived in a matriarchal age that revered the "sacred feminine" as a uniquely divine force?
2. What role has Mary, the Mother of Jesus, played in Christian spirituality?

Questions for Discussion

1. What role does Mary, the Mother of Jesus, play in your spirituality?

seven

STOLEN GODS? CHRISTIANITY AND MYSTERY RELIGIONS

You might have heard this one before:
Christianity's motif of a dying-and-rising god, a water initiation and sacred meal, were by no means unique. You'll find similar myths and practices all around the Mediterranean during this period. We can safely conclude, then, that Christians simply copied their resurrected Son of God, baptism, and Eucharist from what was in the air, to remake what was originally nothing more than a philosophical system into an exciting, attractive new religion.

That would get you thrown to the lions.

Somehow, the perpetrators of this mythology always forget that last part.

Brown presents a version of this in *The Da Vinci Code*. It's short, messy, and pays no heed to evidence, but it can still be disturbing if you take it on face value. Which, of course, you shouldn't.

The Evidence

In *The Da Vinci Code*, our resident scholar Teabing claims that the sacramental system, ritual practices, and symbolism of Christianity as we know it are the result of "transmogrification," or adaptation, of pagan religious symbols and practice by Christians for their own use.

The first problem in Brown's presentation is that he associates all of this — images of "Egyptian sun disks" becoming halos, Isis nursing Horus being adapted to images of Mary nursing Jesus, the act of "God-eating" in communion — with Constantine (of course).

Well, Constantine didn't do any of this. Granted, Constantine's treatment of Christianity and paganism during his reign was, some might say, inconsistent; others might say adaptive. The Sun-God, for example, still had a prominent place on Roman coinage even as Constantine was pouring money into the construction of Christian churches. But he most definitely did not, as Brown says, deliberately fuse "pagan symbols, dates and rituals into the growing Christian tradition" (p. 232).

The question remains: Even if Constantine didn't do it, many Internet sites, and even some books on the subject, would have you believe that there is a suspicious relationship between Christian beliefs and practices and the "mystery religions" that flourished in the ancient Near East during the first four centuries after Christ.

Is Christianity plagiarized?

Mysteries About Mysteries

These mystery religions from which Christianity is supposed to have stolen its practices and beliefs were groups that flourished almost everywhere in the ancient Near East, devoted to various gods, but sharing certain traits.

They were distinct from the officially supported worship of the gods in that they required public fulfillment of religious duties in order to gain divine favor. In fact, most scholars would maintain that these mystery cults flourished because officially sanctioned religion failed to meet any authentic spiritual needs.

The mystery religions emphasized personal salvation, illumination, and eternal life through union with the divine in secret cultic activities. Although diverse, most mystery religions tended to center on uniting the aspiring initiate to the divine through a re-enactment of mythic events, often involving a dying-and-rising deity.

There are a couple of background points to make here before we get into specifics.

Teabing says altars were taken "directly" from mystery religions by Christianity. The truth is that all ancient religions used altars, made of piles of rocks, or wood or stone, for sacrifice. Christians understood the Eucharist to be, in part, a memorial and representation of the sacrifice of Christ. References to altars are found in the New Testament.

First, whenever you think about Christian roots, what you must always consider first are not any ancient pagan religions or rites, but rather Judaism.

Jesus was Jewish, and the great majority of his followers for the first two decades after his death and resurrection were Jewish. The fundamentals of Christian belief about Jesus, and even Christian practice, were laid down in those first two decades, as the letters of Paul, written between the years A.D. 50 and 60, attest.

So, are you startled by the attempt to link Christian baptism with ritual washings of mystery religions? Remember that ritual purification in water and for converts was an established element of Jewish practice at the time of Jesus. Remember what John the Baptist, no follower of Mithra, did. He baptized.

And what about the Eucharist? Teabing calls it "God-eating" and suggests this was just, again, a Christian copy of pagan cultic practices. This, of course, completely ignores the fact that as early Christians remembered it, the Last Supper was a Passover meal (according to the Synoptic Gospels. John puts it the day before Passover). It was this Last Supper that they re-enacted in their own eucharistic celebrations, an act that was described in very Jewish terms — new covenant, sacrifice, and so on.

The second point to remember is most of the evidence we have for the practices of mystery religions date from the third through fifth centuries, and most importantly, hardly any archaeological evidence indicating the existence of mystery cults *in first-century Palestine*, the birthplace of Christianity, has been found.

So, if you're confronted with these assertions, push in the other direction. Someone's telling you that Christians simply adapted the Eucharist from pagan communal meals? Really? What's the evidence for cause and effect? Don't accept anything less than texts and artifacts that clearly fit the time and geographical limitations at hand.

Chances are, they won't be able to find any.

The Sun-God

Brown involved the Emperor Constantine in this process of "transmogrification" by saying that in divinizing Jesus, Constantine simply took the established worship of the sun and remade it into the worship of the Son, and there you have it: a Son of God where you previously had that simple "mortal teacher."

As we have seen, the Emperor Constantine did not invent the idea of Jesus' divinity. Christians had described and worshiped Jesus as Lord since the first century. What is true, though, is that during Constantine's reign, official religious expression did honor both the sun god and the Christian Son of God at various times.

In A.D. 274, the Emperor Aurelian had elevated worship of the sun god to new heights, hailing the deity as "Lord of the Roman Empire," and constructing an enormous temple in Rome to his honor (see W.H.C. Frend, *The Rise of Christianity*, p. 440). Over the next few decades, honor to this deity continued, Christians were persecuted, sometimes severely, until Constantine solidified his power in the Western half of the Empire in 312.

Brown, in his stew of mythological meanderings, pulls another pagan deity into the mix beside the sun god as well. Teabing implies that the pagan god Mithras was the model for Christian beliefs about Jesus, claiming that he bore similar titles, and "was buried in a rock tomb, and then resurrected in three days" (*DVC*, p. 232).

Mithras was a god with many forms. By the centuries after Christ, his cult was primarily a mystery religion, popular among men, especially soldiers. Mithraic studies do not find *any* attribution of the titles "Son of God" or "Light of the World," as Brown claims. There is also no mention of a death-resurrection motif in Mithraic mythology. Brown seems to have picked this up from a discredited nineteenth-century historian, who provided no documentation for his assertion. This same historian is the source for the Krishna connection to which Brown alludes. There is not a single story in actual Hindu mythology of Krishna being presented with gold, frankincense, and myrrh at his birth (see Miesel and Olsen, *Cracking the Anti-Catholic Code)*.

Constantine, like all people of his time, believed that his success was attributable to divine powers. It is simply not clear, for most of his reign, how sharply he distinguished between the sun god and the One God of Christianity. As historian W.H.C. Frend puts it, during those years that Constantine was solidifying his rule and stabilizing the Empire, ". . . he did not abandon his allegiance to the Sun god, even though he regarded himself as a servant of the Christian God" (p. 484).

Near the end of his life, however, he seems to have made his choice, and was baptized (not under duress, as Brown claims) before his death in A.D. 337. It was not uncommon for aspiring Christians to wait until near death for baptism during this period, especially those in positions the exercise of which might involve one in sin, such as taking another's life. Post-baptismal sin was viewed very seriously during this time, and penance for serious sin involved near-excommunication from the Christian community.

Brown repeats two specific assertions related to Christianity and the sun god. First, he claims that the choice of December 25 as the date of Christmas was made as a way of supplanting the pagan celebration of the birth of the sun god, a feast instituted by Aurelian.

The evidence of any purposeful link is non-existent, especially since there is no record of Constantine sponsoring a celebration

> A mitre is a shield-shaped headpiece worn by bishops in the
> Western Church. Teabing says it was adopted from mystery reli-
> gions, but mitres were not worn until the eleventh century. In
> the East, the area closest to mystery cults, bishops wear crowns.

of the birth of Jesus on December 25. The first mention of it, we
find, is it being celebrated in Constantinople in A.D. 379 or 380,
from which it gradually spread through the Eastern Church. There
is, in addition, other evidence to suggest, as historian William
Tighe does, that the selection of December 25 as the date of
Christ's birth might actually have been tied to other factors organic
to Christianity.

By the second century, Christians in the West had settled on
March 25 as the date that Jesus was crucified. Using an old Jewish
tradition that the great prophets died on the same day on which they
had been born or conceived, in the West, March 25 also came to be
understood as the day Jesus was conceived by the Holy Spirit in
Mary's womb (still celebrated today as the feast of the Annuncia-
tion). Counting forward nine months, we arrive at December 25.

We don't know for sure, but what is certain is that there is no
evidence directly linking the Aurelian feast to Christmas, which
was first celebrated a century later, after Christianity had become
the official religion of the Roman Empire.

Now What About Sunday?

Brown blithely claims, through Teabing, that Constantine simply
shifted the Christian day of rest and worship from Saturday to the
Day of the Sun.

This is silly. We have ample evidence that Sunday was special
to Christians from the first century. They did not call it that, of

course. In the Book of Revelation, written near the end of the first century, it is called the "the Lord's day" (1:10), and elsewhere it is called the "First Day," or even the "Eighth Day," the latter referring to it as an eighth day of God's creative action.

By the middle of the second century, the Christian pattern of gathering for Eucharist on Sunday, already related in the Acts of the Apostles (see 20:7), was firmly established. Justin Martyr, writing from Rome during this time, describes the weekly eucharistic assembly on this day in great detail (see *First Apology*).

So of course, Constantine did not move Christian worship from Saturday to Sunday. Christians had been worshiping on Sunday for centuries by then. What he *did* do was to make the seven-day week, known and used in some places, the basis for the calendar and then set aside Sunday as a day of rest throughout the Empire. Time had previously been officially marked in the Empire by using three main days during the month as reference points: *kalends* (first); *nones* (seventh); and, of course, *ides* (fifteenth).

Up to this point, Jews and some pagans who honored Saturn had treated Saturday as a day of rest, but Constantine institutionalized Sunday for this purpose on the official Roman calendar. This pleased the Christians to some extent, of course, but their pleasure was probably mitigated by the name Constantine gave the day: *dies Solis*.

Halos were used in ancient art to distinguish gods, and even the emperor. It appears in Christian art in the third and fourth centuries, at first only around figures of Christ, a natural choice for a symbol, considering the association of Christ with light. It is a symbol, like a crown, with no necessary connection to any particular belief system.

So certainly, we see that the Emperor Constantine, intent on unifying the Empire and solidifying his power, seemed to waffle a bit in terms of religion. He made use of symbols when it was useful and hedged his bets, at least during the first decade or so of his reign, after which he traveled a slightly straighter road to Christianity.

However, we do know that what Brown says is not true: Constantine did not make December 25 Christmas, and he did not make Christians shift their day of worship from Saturday to Sunday.

The Deeper Point

Brown would like us to believe that the integrity of religious systems, beliefs, and symbols is dependent on their complete independence from other religious systems, beliefs, and symbols, from beginning to end.

This is simply not the way human religious systems work. There are certain aspects of human life that we all share, and that all seem to have an intrinsic capacity for meaning that evokes the transcendent.

In birth and death, we confront the mystery and miracle of existence and the hope for something more.

In water and oil, we encounter cleansing, and it brings to mind our own need for purification.

In sharing meals, we find nourishment and community.

There are only so many words, so much "stuff" in human life, that we have to help us symbolize and make present the truths that are revealed to us.

The fact that other religions have washing ceremonies and ritual meals says nothing about the truth or validity of Christian practices. There is no evidence to suggest, as Brown does, a direct adaptation of the fundamentals of Christian thought and practice from pagan mystery religions. The roots of Christianity are in Judaism. Because Christianity is embraced and lived out by human beings living in human culture and society, the expression of faith is bound to be dynamic, embracing language and symbolism that makes those beliefs more understandable. Such a dynamic enhances and deepens our understanding and experience of our faith.

It's just common sense. It's the way the world works, and, Christians believe, the way God works within that world.

For Further Reading

The Early Church, by Henry Chadwick, Penguin Books, 1967.

The Rise of Christianity, by W.H.C. Frend, Fortress Press, 1984.

Calendar: Humanity's Epic Struggle to Determine a True and Accurate Year, by David Ewing Duncan, Avon Books, 1998.

Questions for Review

1. What were mystery religions?
2. What does the evidence suggest about the relationship between the Christian symbols and beliefs and pagan symbols and beliefs described in *The Da Vinci Code?*

Questions for Discussion

1. What concrete steps can you take to improve your knowledge of the Jewish roots of the Christian faith?
2. Can you think of parallels to the Christian celebrations of baptism and the Lord's Supper in the Old Testament?

eight

SURELY HE GOT LEONARDO DA VINCI RIGHT?

Actually, no, he didn't.

If you want to know how wrong Brown is about Leonardo da Vinci, you need only consider something quite simple: the artist's name.

Beginning with the title, and continuing throughout the novel, Brown and all of his expert characters refer to this artist as "Da Vinci."

Well, guess what? *That's not his name.*

Nowhere in historical or educational literature is he referred to that way.

His name was "Leonardo" and he was born, the illegitimate son of one Piero da Vinci, in 1452 in the town of Vinci, which is not far from Florence. So obviously, "da Vinci" means "of Vinci."

Someone claiming to have expertise in art and who consistently refers to him as "Da Vinci" is just as credible as a supposed religion expert calling Jesus "of Nazareth."

Pick up any art history book. You'll read about Leonardo, not "Da Vinci." Go to the library and look for a biography of the artist. You will not find it under "D" or "V." You will find it under "L" for Leonardo because that is his name.

So perhaps we can agree on this: An author who can't even get the name of the central historical figure in his book right shouldn't be trusted to teach us history. He can entertain us in other ways, but let us please not even for a second allow *The Da Vinci Code* to form our ideas about history, religion, or even art.

Who Was Leonardo?

Leonardo is, of course, one of the most intriguing intellectual figures in Western history. His body of work and thinking could
provide the fodder for many novels, but the real Leonardo, as we
understand him, bears little resemblance to how Brown presents
him.

He claims that Leonardo was a "flamboyant homosexual and
worshipper of Nature's divine order, both of which placed him in
a perpetual state of sin against God" (*DVC*, p. 45).

According to Brown, Leonardo had an "enormous output of
breathtaking Christian art," hundreds of commissions from the Vatican, although in constant conflict with the Church (see *DVC*, p. 45).

Actually, the only perpetual conflict with "the church" Leonardo
had concerned his tendency to leave work he had contracted for
unfinished. But that's another matter.

The general picture we gather from *The Da Vinci Code* is of a
defiant genius, obsessed with his rejection of Christianity, working
this rejection into his enormous outpouring of work. (Oh, and also
of a grand master of the Priory of Sion, an organization, we will see
in the next chapter, that probably never existed, especially in the form
and for the reasons Brown suggests.)

This portrait doesn't quite capture what Leonardo was really
about, especially in the context of his time.

Let's take the tabloid material first. Was Leonardo a "flamboyant homosexual?" There's no evidence that he was. In 1476, he was,
along with three others, charged with sodomy with a well-known
male prostitute in Florence. The charges were dismissed.

That's the only mention of possible homosexual activity — or any
sexual activity — related to Leonardo in any primary sources related
to his life, including his own voluminous notebooks. As Sherwin B.
Nuland writes in his biography of Leonardo, *Leonardo da Vinci*:

"The episode is the only hint of sexual activity by Leonardo,
and those who have been the most painstaking students of his life
assume it never happened" (p. 31).

Or, as art historian Bruce Boucher says, writing in *The New York Times* in 2003, ". . . despite a charge of sodomy against him as a young man, the evidence of his sexual orientation remains inconclusive and fragmentary."

Now for that enormous output of breathtaking Christian art. Perhaps Brown is privy to some secret information here, because what has survived, even in preliminary drawings, reflects, at best, a couple of dozen paintings on Christian themes. And certainly there were no "hundreds of Vatican commissions." Leonardo worked under the patronage of only one Pope, Leo X, near the end of his life, and spent the time occupied with scientific experiments.

Indeed, when we look at the work of Leonardo in terms of quantity, it is not paintings that stand out; it is the hundreds of drawings, engineering, and architectural schemas, the scientific experiments and the inventions. To characterize Leonardo as a figure primarily engaged in turning out paintings on Christian themes with hidden anti-Christian messages encoded is ludicrous, first of all because paintings on Christian themes did not even seem to be the focus of his work.

Leonardo: Heretic?

In *The Da Vinci Code*, Leonardo is explained as some sort of spiritual radical who gleefully thumbs his nose at Christian tradition in his subversive use of symbols in his art. Before we decide to be shocked and intrigued by this, let's put Leonardo's spiritual beliefs in perspective.

Leonardo da Vinci lived in Italy and (for a short time) in France during the period of the Renaissance. "Renaissance" means "rebirth" and refers, not to the rebirth of culture in general, as so many believe, but more specifically to the rebirth of *classical* culture — the philosophy, writing, art, and general sensibility of ancient Greece and Rome. One of the consequences of the Crusades — the continuing wars between the Christian West and the aggressive Muslim East — was a rediscovery of these works, as Crusaders brought back manuscripts and art they had looted from the East, where they had been preserved.

Leonardo lived in a period of brilliant, swirling, intellectual activity focused on the natural world and the life of human beings in this natural world, enriched by encounters with Greek and Roman culture. You shouldn't assume, though, that this activity necessarily stood in opposition to the Christian Church. It didn't. The Church was still the prime locus of intellectual activity during this time, all universities were Church-sponsored, and many of the intellectuals exploring classical culture in their contemporary context were, indeed, clerics — priests, monks, and even bishops.

Leonardo was born and lived in a culture still defined by a Catholic Christian framework, but it is clear from his notebooks that he was not, in any way, a believer in traditional Catholic practices. He does, however, write about God and even Christ. Serge Bramly writes in his biography of Leonardo, *Leonardo: The Artist and the Man*:

"He believed in God — though not perhaps a very Christian God. . . . He discovered this God in the miraculous beauty of light, in the harmonious movement of the planets, in the intricate arrangement of muscles and nerves inside the body, and that inexpressible masterpiece the human soul. . . . Leonardo was probably not a practicing worshiper; or rather he practiced in his own way. His art remained essentially religious through and through. Even in a profane [non-religious] work, Leonardo was celebrating the sublime creation of the Almighty, which he sought to understand and reflect" (p. 281).

Leonardo was, however, seriously anti-clerical. He criticized the wealth of some clerics, the exploitation of credulous and fearful believers, as well as the selling of indulgences and elaborate honor given to saints.

Living just before the Reformation exploded in Europe (Martin Luther nailed his *95 Theses* to the door of the Wittenberg church in 1517, two years before Leonardo's death), Leonardo expressed thoughts that were very common, especially in intellectual circles, and even among more observant and pious Catholics who were distressed by excesses they observed in the lives of Church leaders.

So, Leonardo, while remarkable and unique in his genius, wasn't really as radical in his spiritual beliefs as Brown would like you to think. In some ways, he was very much a man of his time: open to exploring the world any way he could, using the natural world and human experience as a beginning and reference point for his exploration, a believer in God, and, it seems, Christ, but deeply anti-clerical and disdainful of excesses in piety and religious expression.

Now let's get to those paintings.

The Madonna of the Rocks

In *The Da Vinci Code*, Leonardo's two versions of *The Madonna of the Rocks*, one in the Louvre, and one in the National Gallery in London, supposedly tell the story of a Leonardo intent on communicating anti-Christian secrets.

Well, a simple examination of the paintings in question show how wrongheaded Brown's contention is.

Leonardo first received the commission to paint this picture as a part of an altarpiece for the chapel of a group called the Confraternity of the Immaculate Conception. Brown declares this to be a group of nuns.

No. A "confraternity," particularly during this time, was a group of men who organized themselves for a purpose, in this case to promote the belief in Mary's Immaculate Conception (the teaching that God preserved Mary from original sin from the beginning of her life). Nuns are women, not men.

The confraternity gave detailed instructions for what they wanted: Mary in the center, clad in gold, blue and green, flanked by two prophets, with God the Father overhead, the Child on a golden platform (see Bramly, p. 184). (Note that this is not at all what Brown says about the details of the contract on page 138.) The commission was made in 1483, but over the next twenty-five years, Leonardo and the confraternity engaged in a protracted battle about the painting.

The battle does not seem to have anything to do with the details Brown mentions, although it's clear that Leonardo's more naturalistic style was not going to incorporate the aspects the confraternity wanted. No, although the details are somewhat mysterious, the conflict seems to be more about payment — Leonardo repeatedly asked for more money, which the confraternity was unwilling to give.

And why are there two versions? It seems that at one point, the original was given away. Some say the ruler of Milan, Ludovico Sforza, gave it to either the French king or the German emperor — and this is the version that is in the Louvre. The second version, which is in London, was taken directly from the chapel, which no longer exists.

Let's look at what Brown says is so shocking about these paintings. He claims that in them John the Baptist is blessing Jesus, rather than the other way around, which is what you would expect.

Well, here's the truth: In both versions, Jesus is blessing John the Baptist.

What evidently tricks Brown up is that in the painting, John the Baptist is close to Mary and she has her arm around him. But, there is no art scholar who thinks that the baby kneeling there with his hands folded isn't John the Baptist. It is an unusual arrangement, but as is doubly clear from the London version, where John is wearing a little animal skin and holds the staff always associated with him in iconography, it's John who's being blessed.

And as for the rest of the painting in the Louvre? Mary's hand hovering over Jesus is certainly a bit of a mystery, but seems to imply a sense of protection. The angel's hand is not menacing — it is pointing to John the Baptist, as the prophet to whom we should listen.

It is an unusual painting, particularly given the commission. Its relationship to the Immaculate Conception would certainly have been murky to his patrons. However, as Bramly points out, it is definitely possible to see a relation:

"The Immaculate Conception, Leonardo seems to be saying, paves the way for the agony of the cross ..." (p. 190).

Brown, then, gets the identity of Leonardo's patron and the major figures in the painting wrong, misrepresents the nature of the conflict, and misinterprets the painting.

The Adoration of the Magi

Our hero Langdon at one point tries to explain Leonardo's mysterious controversial messages in his art by alluding to *The Adoration of the Magi*, in the Uffizi Gallery in Florence. He cites a *New York Times Magazine* story (an authentic reference — April 21, 2001, was the publication date) highlighting the work of Maurizio Seracini, an art historian who had supposedly uncovered tremendous secrets hidden in the work.

The Adoration of the Magi is a preparatory drawing for a painting commissioned by a monastery in Florence. The drawing is as far, most scholars believe, as Leonardo got, before he moved to Milan. There is a layer of painting over the drawing that, Seracini claims, hides what Leonardo originally drew. There was an enormous conflict about removing this top layer, as Brown says.

However, he's completely wrong on the reason. It's not because of anything revealed in the drawing — proprietors of museums in largely secularized Italy do not have a great fear of potentially anti-religious or heretical sentiments in art. No, the controversy stemmed from a more fundamental division in the art world between those dedicated to restoring art to its original state, and those opposed.

In this case, once the plans for the restoration — the removal of the top layer — were announced, many people in the art world, led by a group called Art Watch International, voiced strong protests. They said that the work was too fragile for such a restoration, there was no absolute proof that Leonardo had not done this top layer himself, and it wasn't an attempt to fill in color, but a preparatory layer on which the rest of the paint would go. They dispute the assumption that the preparatory layer cannot have been from Leonardo's hand.

In short, Art Watch claimed that restoration would damage the work on a number of levels. They won, and plans for the restoration were halted in 2002, but not for the reasons Brown suggests (for more, see www.artwatchinternational.org).

The Mona Lisa

In *The Da Vinci Code,* Langdon recalls a lecture he gave to prisoners in which he explains the *Mona Lisa* in terms of androgyny: that the painting, which computerized analysis shows, has points of congruity with Leonardo's self-portraits, is a purposefully androgynous picture of a male-female figure, reflecting Leonardo's ideal of a balance between masculine and feminine. Even the name "Mona Lisa" is an anagram of the names of Egyptian deities of fertility: Amon (male) and Isis (female).

We've got a few points to make here:

The identity of the subject in the *Mona Lisa*, also called "*La Gioconda*," painted between 1503 and 1505, is certainly mysterious. There are dozens of theories, none of them really provable. One of those theories, the oldest, in fact, is that it is a painting of a real woman, Monna (or Mona) Lisa, the wife of a Florentine named Francesco del Giocondo.

There are, according to art historian Bruce Boucher in *The New York Times*, "no definitively documented images of Leonardo" to which anyone could compare this painting, and Bramly calls the self-portrait theory the "most far-fetched" (p. 369).

Amon (or Ammon or Amun) was an Egyptian sun god who, despite its sometimes impressive phallic representation, was not particularly associated with fertility. If he is associated with any female deity it is not Isis, but Muth.

Besides, any relationship between the names of Egyptian gods, Leonardo, and this painting can be immediately and easily discounted when we understand one simple point: Leonardo did not name this painting. He does not even mention the painting in any of his notebooks, although there is no doubt it is his work. The portrait is identified as *Mona Lisa* by Leonardo's first biographer, Giorgio Visari, writing some three decades after Leonardo's death. His is the only reference we find to the portrait's identification as "*Mona Lisa*"; the title is nowhere mentioned by Leonardo himself. So, how could he have been communicating something through the title he himself, apparently, had nothing to do with (see Bramly, p. 368).

The Last Supper

Here, at last, we get to the heart of the matter. Is *The Last Supper* full of codes pointing to a married Jesus and Mary Magdalene and an enraged Peter?

Brown claims that in this painting Leonardo communicated his knowledge that Jesus and Mary Magdalene were married, that she was to be the leader of his Church, that Peter did not approve, and that she was the real Holy Grail.

Why? Because the figure understood as John is really Mary. The position of Jesus and Mary formed an "M," a disembodied hand, supposedly Peter's, wielded a knife, and there is no chalice. So the chalice must be Mary.

First, let's do a little background. *The Last Supper* is painted on the wall of a refectory (dining room) in a monastery in Milan. It is not, as Brown states, a fresco. A fresco is a painting executed with water based pigments on moist lime plaster, which then "traps" the paint as it dries and produces strong colors and a lasting effect. Leonardo worked too slowly to use fresco, and he wanted to try something different, so he put a thin base on the stone wall and used tempera paint on top of that. It was a miserable choice, for even a few years after the mural was complete, paint had begun to fade and flake off.

In order to properly understand this painting, it's important to see that it's not about simply the Last Supper in general. It's about a specific moment, based on a particular Scripture passage.

When we think of the Last Supper, we naturally associate it with the Institution of the Eucharist. Brown plays on this expectation, pointing out that there is no central chalice or central loaf of bread in the painting. The absence of the chalice, he says, implies that Mary is the real Grail, and so on.

The problem with this is that the particular subject of this painting is not the moment of the Institution of the Eucharist. Instead, it concerns the moment at which Jesus has announced that someone will betray him, as specifically described in the Gospel of John 13:21-24:

"When he had said this, Jesus was deeply troubled and testified, 'Amen, amen, I say to you, one of you will betray me.' The disciples looked at one another, at a loss as to whom he meant. One of his disciples, the one whom Jesus loved, was reclining at Jesus' side So Simon Peter nodded to him to find out whom he meant. He leaned back against Jesus' chest and said to him, 'Master, who is it?' "

Leonardo intended for each of the figures to express a particular response to that announcement of betrayal. It is a supremely dramatic moment, with the apostles all leaning away from Jesus, leaving him, in a way, isolated (as they would later), speaking with one another, wondering who the betrayer could be, and including the image of Peter speaking to John. But it is not about the Institution of the Eucharist, for the Gospel of John, unlike the Synoptic Gospels, contains no direct account of the Institution of the Eucharist, hence, no chalice is necessary in this particular representation.

Is the figure whom we all believe to be John really Mary?

No. During this time, St. John was invariably represented as a beautiful young man. He may look feminine to us, but to people

Why is there no account of the institution of the Eucharist in John? Most scholars believe that by the time this Gospel was written, late in the first century, the Christian sense that the details of their most sacred rituals should only be known to the fully initiated. This is why, for example, early Christian converts did not have the word of the Lord's Prayer revealed to them until a week or two before their baptisms, and certainly did not participate in the entire liturgy until after they were initiated. It is assumed that John's Gospel expresses that practice.

of the period, he was clearly a male, seated, as St. John always was in representations of the scene, at Jesus' side.

Art historian Elizabeth Levy helps us understand this in greater depth:

"Brown capitalizes on Leonardo's soft-featured, beardless depiction of John to offer his fantastic claim that we are dealing with a woman. Of course, if St. John were really Mary Magdalene, we may well ask which of the apostles excused himself at the critical moment. The real problem stems from our lack of familiarity with "types." In his *Treatise on Painting*, Leonardo explains that each figure should be painted according to his station and age. A wise man has certain characteristics, an old woman others, and children others still. A classic type, common to many Renaissance paintings, is the "student." A favored follower, a protégé, or disciple, is always portrayed as very youthful, long-haired, and clean-shaven; the idea being that he has not yet matured to the point where he must find his own way. Throughout the Renaissance, artists portray St. John in this fashion. He is the "disciple Jesus loved" — the only one who will be at the foot of the cross. He is the ideal student. To the Renaissance artist, the only way to show

St. John was as a beardless youth, with none of the hard, determined physiognomy of men. The *Last Supper* of Ghirlandaio and Andrea del Castagno show a similarly soft, young John" (from an article on www.zenit.org). As art historian Bruce Boucher notes in an article in the August 3, 2003 *New York Times*, the mysterious disembodied hand that Brown claims is menacing Mary/John has an explanation as well:

". . . yet this hand is not disembodied. Both a preliminary drawing by Leonardo and early copies of *The Last Supper* show that the hand and dagger belong to Peter — a reference to a passage in the Gospel of St. John in which Peter draws a sword in defense of Jesus."

So yes, *The Last Supper* is an evocative painting, rich with possibilities for contemplating, for example, our own reactions to Jesus as we consider the apostles' varied responses to him. But it does not say anything Brown suggests it does. The evidence is simply not there.

And don't forget — it's Leonardo.

For Further Reading

Leonardo da Vinci, by Sherwin B. Nuland, Viking Press, 2000.

Leonardo: The Artist and the Man, by Serge Bramley, Penguin Books, 1995.

Inventing Leonardo, by Richard Turner, Knopf, 1993.

Questions for Review

1. What kind of person was Leonardo? What was the focus of his work?
2. What is the meaning and symbolism in *The Last Supper?*

Questions for Discussion

1. How can art help a person to meditate upon the life of Christ?
2. What does art teach us about how the Gospel message is lived out in different epochs?

nine

THE GRAIL, THE PRIORY, AND THE KNIGHTS TEMPLAR

The history of the image of the Holy Grail is ambiguous and mysterious, easily lending itself to mythology, fantasy, and romance. It has played an important role in legend (the King Arthur legends), poetry (*The Idylls of the King,* by Alfred Lord Tennyson) and, of course, opera (Richard Wagner's *Parsifal* and *Lohengrin*).

So, seen in that perspective, one can't blame Brown for picking up the theories from *Holy Blood, Holy Grail* and *The Templar Revelation* and using them in a novel. It may be offensive to some, but the act of using the image in such a way is consistent with its use throughout history.

However, it's still worth discussing, because the effect of *The Da Vinci Code* is to cross the line between obvious fiction and possible fact. He throws intelligent-sounding evidence at his readers on every page, and we're left wondering if he's right.

Is there any kind of substantial tradition of seeing the Holy Grail as Mary Magdalene and her womb? Is this really what the Knights Templar and Priory of Sion were all about?

In a word, no.

The Holy Grail

The origins of the Holy Grail legend are obscure, perhaps lying deep in the mists of Celtic legends about life-giving vessels of blood. Our first and one of the greatest written texts about the Grail is in the medieval poem, *Perceval,* by Chrètien de Troyes, who lived in the twelfth century.

In this and in other legends of the period, the precise identification of exactly what the Grail is varies. It is a beautiful jeweled vessel, capable of bestowing unlimited food and drink. It was the dish from which Jesus and the apostles ate the Paschal lamb, it was the cup Jesus used at the Last Supper, and it was the vessel in which Joseph of Arimathea caught the blood of Christ as it poured from his body on the cross.

In legend, the Grail is often protected by a woman, and its existence is the reason for many a quest. The Grail legends are a mix of folklore, romance, and religious mythology. Although there are a few cups around the world that claim to be the Holy Grail, as the cup of Jesus at the Last Supper, the Church has never formally incorporated Grail lore into its tradition.

Because of the role of women in protecting the Grail, as well as instances in which the Grail bears the image of a child on it, the Grail does, indeed, carry some symbolism related to child-bearing and life-giving. However, there is no known tradition explicitly equating, as Brown says, the Grail with symbols of the "lost goddess," Mary Magdalene, or the bloodline of Jesus (as the authors of *Holy Blood, Holy Grail* put it). And, most scholars understand this imagery, when used in a Christian context, to be evocative of the Virgin Mary, to whom devotion exploded during the early Middle Ages.

And as for that terribly exciting, shocking moment at the end of chapter fifty-eight, when Teabing breaks down the French word *Sangreal*? He claims the traditional etymology breaks it into *san Greal* or "Holy Grail," but ah, no — let's see what happens when we break it down into *Sang Real*: It means Royal Blood! Proof!

I have before me an article on the Holy Grail from the 1914 edition of the *Catholic Encyclopedia*. It says:

"The explanation of 'San greal' as 'sang real' (kingly blood), was not current until the later Middle Ages."

Royal blood, in the context of traditional Grail stories is, of course, the blood of Christ. That particular breakdown of the word wasn't big news in the late Middle Ages or in 1914, and it's not big news now.

The Knights Templar and the Priory of Sion

The story that Brown tells about the Knights Templar and the Priory of Sion are based on the material from, if we even need to repeat ourselves, *Holy Blood, Holy Grail* and *The Templar Revelation*. Most of what he says about them has no basis in fact.

First, it's important to understand that, in contrast to what Brown says in the front of his book, the Priory of Sion was *not* a real organization in the way that Brown describes it. The documents he cites, along with that famous list of grand masters, including Victor Hugo and, of course, Leonardo, are forgeries, placed in the French National Library, probably in the late 1950s.

Very briefly, the story is this:

There seems to be evidence of a Priory of Sion emerging in late nineteenth-century France, a right-wing group dedicated to fighting representative government.

The name comes again right before World War II, in the efforts of a man named Pierre Plantard. Plantard was an anti-Semite who sought to "purify and renew" France. In the mid-1950s, Plantard started claiming he was the heir to the French throne, from the Merovingian line. He formed a group called the "Priory of Sion," planted false documents attesting to its antiquity in French libraries and archives, and propagated the "royal bloodline of Jesus" myth.

As Laura Miller concludes in an article in *The New York Times* ("The Da Vinci Con," February 22, 2004):

"Finally, though, the legitimacy of the Priory of Sion history rests on a cache of clippings and pseudonymous documents that even the authors of *Holy Blood, Holy Grail* suggest were planted in the Bibliotheque Nationale by a man named Pierre Plantard. As early as the 1970's, one of Plantard's confederates had admitted to helping him fabricate the materials, including genealogical tables portraying Plantard as a descendant of the Merovingians (and, presumably, of Jesus Christ) and a list of the Priory's past 'grand masters.' This patently silly catalog of intellectual celebrities stars Botticelli, Isaac Newton, Jean Cocteau and, of course, Leonardo da Vinci — and it's the same list Dan Brown trumpets, along with the alleged nine-century pedigree of the Priory, in the front matter for *The Da Vinci Code*, under the heading of 'Fact.' Plantard, it eventually came out, was an inveterate rascal with a criminal record for fraud and affiliations with wartime anti-Semitic and right-wing groups. The actual Priory of Sion was a tiny, harmless group of like-minded friends formed in 1956.

"Plantard's hoax was debunked by a series of (as yet untranslated) French books and a 1996 BBC documentary, but curiously enough, this set of shocking revelations hasn't proved as popular as the fantasia of *Holy Blood, Holy Grail*, or, for that matter, as *The Da Vinci Code*."

Saint-Sulpice: In *The Da Vinci Code*, the Church of Saint-Sulpice (built 1646-1789) in Paris is used by the Priory of Sion to hide a secret associated with the Grail. The mythical history of the never-existent priory draws this association, but there is, in truth, none. The "Rose Line" and obelisk have no esoteric meaning. The true story is that a surprising number of European churches doubled as astronomical observatories. A small hole was made in the ceiling or a wall, and the movement of the sun was tracked along a line on the floor. When the sun reached a certain point, in this case, the obelisk, it was either the winter or summer solstice. (For more on this subject, see *The Sun in the Church*, by J. L. Heilbron, Harvard University Press, 1999.)

So, simply put, the Priory of Sion as a thousand-year group dedicated to protecting the Grail never existed.

The Knights Templar, however, did exist. They were founded in the Holy Land after the conquest of Jerusalem in the eleventh century. The Knights, also called the Poor Knights of Christ and of the Temple of Solomon, were a monastic order of knights. They were "monastic" in the sense that they took vows — primarily to protect the Holy Land sacred sites and pilgrims journeying there — and lived in obedience to a rule that outlined religious obligations (daily prayer and Mass, led by priests of the order), and requirements for behavior:

"Some of the instructions seemed precisely to be aimed at limiting the excesses of knightly behavior. They were to be humble men with limited resources.... There was to be no jousting, and they were not to go hunting" (*The Warriors of the Lord*, by Michael Walsh, p. 156).

The Knights Templar grew in power during the thirteenth and fourteenth centuries, along with other military orders, including its main rival, the Hospitallers. They amassed great wealth, and acted as a banking house in both Paris and London.

Did the Knights Templar have any relationship with the legend of the Grail? Not until the nineteenth century, it seems, when interest in secret societies grew, especially in relation to Freemasonry. In 1818, a German named Joseph von Hammer-Purgstall wrote a book called *Mystery of Baphomet Revealed*, in which he outlined a purported history of the Knights Templar that included them worshiping Mohammed and being guardians of the Holy Grail, which in his version was not the cup of the Last Supper but some sort of Gnostic knowledge and, particularly, "a special brand of Gnostics who had cursed Christ" (Walsh, p. 190). Modern speculation about the Knights clearly has its roots in this kind of writing.

Back to real history. The Knights were certainly suppressed, but Brown does not get the details quite right.

He places the blame on Pope Clement V, but the evidence indicates pretty clearly that it was the French King Philip II who decided to take on the Templars, mostly because he was broke and they possessed a great deal of wealth. He made the first move, on October 13, 1307. King Philip ordered all Templars in France to be arrested — not "across Europe," as Brown says, although he is correct about the subsequent association of this date, Friday the 13th, with bad luck.

Pope Clement was angered by Philip's action because the Knights were under his protection, but then, on November 22, he acceded to pressure and agreed to the continent-wide crackdown.

> **Did the Knights Templar invent and propagate Gothic architecture as a means of communicating the importance of the "sacred feminine"? No. There's no record of the Knights Templar being involved in architecture, except the construction of their own churches. The Gothic style was developed and perfected from 1100 to 1500, first in France, as an exploration of ways to construct stronger and higher church walls, arches, and allowing as much light in as possible. Gothic structures are rich with symbolism, but a conscious, explicit imitation of female anatomy isn't an element.**

In discussing the Templars, Brown frequently refers to "the Vatican" as the source of papal decisions. Once again, he's wrong in a way that betrays a fundamental unfamiliarity with the period. During these years, Pope Clement V did not live in the Vatican, and not even in Italy. He lived in Avignon, France, a virtual prisoner of King Philip II, under tremendous pressure to do the king's bidding.

The Templars were finally dissolved in 1312 by the Council of Vienne, which, at first, had been hesitant to do anything, but then took action when Philip appeared suddenly at the city gates. The condemnation, as writer Michael Walsh puts it, "was only provisional, and did not accept the Templars' guilt" (p. 173).

Ironically, the Templars' property was given to the other major military order, the Hospitallers. King Philip failed to prosper from his brutal actions, and died, as did Pope Clement V, within a year.

So, in terms of the Templars, Brown vastly overstates the antipathy of Pope Clement V for the group, and fails to lay the blame in its proper place: on King Philip of France.

Finally, Brown gets one more important point very wrong. He claims that the circular design of the Temple Church in London is pagan, built because the Templars chose to "ignore" traditional Church architecture and instead honor the sun.

Considering that the Knights Templar were, by every scrap of evidence, a *Catholic* group whose members vowed loyalty to defend the Catholic faith, that is highly unlikely. Moreover, it's wrong, because the round Temple Church was, quite logically, built in imitation of a church in a city of great importance to the Knights Templar: The Church of the Holy Sepulchre, marking the traditional burial spot of Jesus, in Jerusalem.

Which is, of course, round.

It's worth adding that "the Vatican" was not even the primary papal residence during this time, even if Clement had been there. From the fourth century to the early fourteenth century, the papal residence was at the Lateran. It was destroyed by fire in 1308, right before the captivity in Avignon, and it was only when the papacy returned to Rome in 1377 that they took up residence in the Vatican.

For Further Reading

The Grail: From Celtic Myth to Christian Symbol, by Roger Sherman Loomis, Princeton University Press, 1991.

The Warriors of the Lord: The Military Orders of Christendom, by Michael Walsh, William B. Eerdmans Publishing, 2003.

Questions for Review

1. What does legend suggest about the image of the Holy Grail?
2. What role did the Knights Templar play in Christian history?

Question for Discussion

1. What do you think the appeal of the Holy Grail legend is?

ten

THE CATHOLIC CODE

As you finish reading *The Da Vinci Code*, you emerge with a definite, and not so flattering, image of the Roman Catholic Church.

Sure, the novel tries to occasionally cover its bases as it declares that the modern Catholic Church certainly wouldn't engage in dastardly deeds, because, gosh, it's done so much good. Even though it's done so much evil. And, in the end, of course, the Catholic bad guys are exposed to not be bad guys at all (except for the killing part), but really dupes of Teabing, who's revealed to be the mysterious "Teacher" pulling everyone's strings.

But this twist doesn't do anything to diminish the overall effect of the novel, which is that the Roman Catholic Church is a monolithic, tightly controlled institution devoted to propagating a fiction to a world that yearns to be free.

It's not an uncommon image of the Catholic Church in pop culture, and not one limited to recent history, either. Read any of the wealth of nineteenth-century American anti-Catholic verbal and pictorial propaganda. Same stuff, only in more flowery language and with more blatantly scary pointy-hatted clerics.

It's an image that courses through *The Da Vinci Code*, most vividly in its portrait of the group Opus Dei.

Opus Dei

These days, it almost seems as if Opus Dei has been selected to play the role in contemporary culture that the Jesuit order used to represent, and for centuries: a tightly organized group, directly controlled by the Vatican, that's infiltrating the world's institutions in order to gain power and do . . . something.

The Jesuits, founded by St. Ignatius Loyola in 1534 as a missionary and teaching order, were, in fact, so highly suspect that they were tossed out of several European countries in the late eighteenth century, and even suppressed by the pope in some areas from 1773 to 1814. The order's supposed dark deeds have been prominent in anti-Catholic literature from both secular and Protestant sources, and even today. "Jesuitical" is not a complementary term.

In that sense, as a symbol in the popular mind for secrecy and evil masquerading as good, Opus Dei certainly, and unfortunately, has replaced the Jesuit order.

Now, there are certainly people who have had negative experiences with Opus Dei. They speak of feeling manipulated into membership and excessively controlled once they were involved. In drawing a complete picture of Opus Dei, it's important to listen to these people and take their stories seriously. But it's striking that the only sources Brown draws upon in describing Opus Dei in *The Da Vinci Code* are negative and disillusioned accounts. That's only one side of the story — an important one — but still, one side only.

In *The Da Vinci Code*, Brown gets a few things right about Opus Dei. Yes, they do have a large, relatively new headquarters in New York City. Yes, its members are devoted to traditional piety. Yes, it is a personal prelature (we'll explain that in a minute).

And yes, some members practice corporal mortification.

But that's about it.

First of all, let's clear up one huge error. Silas, our towering albino killer, is described as a "monk." He wears robes, too, to prove it.

Opus Dei does not have "monks."

It's not a religious order, first of all, like Dominicans, Benedictines, or (yes) the Jesuits. Any monks you find in Roman Catholicism belong to religious orders, and live in monasteries or hermitages.

Opus Dei is an association of lay people and priests. There are far more lay members of Opus Dei than clergy, for it was first established for laity in 1928. It was only fifteen years later that the

A "monk" is a man who withdraws from society in order to dedicate himself to God through prayer. Women who pursue the monastic life are called "nuns."

Priestly Society of the Holy Cross was established, formally incorporating priests into the work of Opus Dei.

The founder of Opus Dei was Josemaría Escrivá de Balaguer, a Spanish priest. He established the group as a means for lay people to live out their own unique call to holiness in the world, and grow in love for God and all people. Father Escriva's first and most popular book, in which one can find the spirit of Opus Dei (which means "work of God"), is called *The Way*. Father Escriva's teachings are available in other books as well, including *Christ is Passing By*, from which this passage comes:

"The fact that Jesus grew up and lived just like us shows us that human existence and all the ordinary activity of men have a divine meaning. No matter how much we may have reflected on all this, we should always be surprised when we think of the thirty years of obscurity which made up the greater part of Jesus' life among men. He lived in obscurity, but, for us, that period is full of light. It illuminates our days and fills them with meaning, for we are ordinary Christians who lead an ordinary life, just like millions of other people all over the world" (p. 94).

That passage aptly summarizes the spirit of Opus Dei, and also serves to correct those who, once again, have been convinced by Brown that traditional Christianity is all about ignoring Jesus' human nature and the realities of human life.

Father Escriva died in 1975 and was canonized a saint on October 6, 2002.

Of course, it's not this spirit of Opus Dei that intrigues people, or even strikes them as strange. It's other aspects of the group's life, aspects that Brown plays off of in *The Da Vinci Code*.

Opus Dei does have different levels of membership, but what this reflects are simply varied levels of commitment and different lifestyles. All Opus Dei members follow the same "plan of life" under the guidance of a spiritual director that involves the Rosary, daily Mass, spiritual reading, and mental prayer. Some, however, do this in the context of married life — supernumeraries. Numerary members may still work in the world, but they commit to celibacy, turn most of their salaries over to Opus Dei, and often live in community in Opus Dei houses. There are other members, all of whom have their unique role in "the work."

And what is the work? It is simply living out God's call in the world as deeply as one can. That may involve holding a profession in the world, or it may involve participation in one of Opus Dei's many ministries around the world: schools of all types, agricultural training programs in poor countries, clinics, and other institutions.

One of the more controversial aspects to Opus Dei is one that is frequently highlighted in *The Da Vinci Code*: corporeal, or physical mortification, through the use of the cilice, a spiked chain worn around the thigh, and use of the discipline, a knotted rope for whipping.

This practice certainly seems odd to many modern people, but it might be useful to note that bodily mortification, as a spiritual practice, is found in *every world religion* in some form or another:

Opus Dei is a "personal prelature," which means that the ministries it undertakes are under the authority of the group's own bishop, not the bishop of the diocese in which that work is undertaken. In this way, it is somewhat similar to a religious order, like the Benedictines or Dominicans.

fasting, sometimes to extreme levels, praying or meditating in uncomfortable positions, and even the purposeful wearing of uncomfortable clothes or going without shoes.

Bodily spiritual mortification, including the use of these particular devices, was not invented by Opus Dei, either. If you read the lives of the saints, you find that many felt called to these practices. Why?

Some sought to draw closer to Christ by sharing in his sufferings. Some used them as a means of penance for their own sins or the sins of others. Others saw them as an effective means for growing in self-discipline, seeking to reach a point at which their spirit could focus on God and be content with God's presence, no matter what bodily discomforts they might be experiencing.

It is unusual, but to attain some perspective, you might compare it to the "bodily mortifications" some of us endure for the sake of our physical appearance: fasting, enduring pain as we exercise, and even submitting to procedures — surgeries — that draw blood and cause pain. All for the sake of appearance, which means, in essence, what others see when they look at us.

One who has experienced spiritual growth would argue that "no pain, no gain" applies to the spiritual life, too, at least for them.

There is also an air of secrecy around Opus Dei that encourages speculation because certain aspects of it are secret. For example, Opus Dei publishes no membership lists and discourages members from announcing their membership.

The reason, they would say, is not because anything bad is going on, but out of a sense of humility and obedience to the Gospel. Jesus, in the Gospel of Matthew (see 6:1-18) instructs his followers to live in holiness but to do so almost in secrecy. If you give alms, he says, "do not let your left hand know what your right hand is doing." When you pray, go in your inner room, close the door, and pray. When you fast, do not look gloomy (and, we can assume, hungry!). Wash your face, Jesus says, and anoint your head, so that you don't look as if you are fasting.

It's in that spirit that Opus Dei members keep their spiritual practices and association low-key. Their call, as they understand it, is to be leaven and quiet light in the world, simply living out "the way" as they do the work of God in their daily lives.

The Only Christians?

In a way, Roman Catholics reading *The Da Vinci Code* should be flattered. After all, according to Brown's vision of past and present, the only embodiment of Christianity the world has seen is the Roman Catholic Church.

This is, of course, not quite the case. For example, much of the theological action we've covered in this book — the formation of the Canon, the discussions of Jesus' human and divine nature — was centered, not in the West, but in the East, and involved mostly Eastern bishops. Eastern Catholic and Eastern Orthodox Churches embody that ancient tradition just as deeply as the Roman Catholic Church does.

And then, of course, there are the Christian churches that emerged in the wake of the Reformation, which despite deep differences with Catholicism and Orthodoxy on issues ranging from justification and salvation to sacraments, still continued to affirm the traditional doctrinal understanding of Jesus' human and divine nature as found in those early creeds, understandings that Teabing asserts violate the "original history" of Jesus. Some also engaged in just as much heretic and witch-hammering as the Roman Catholic Church (Catholic bishops, for example, weren't in charge in seventeenth-century Salem, Massachusetts).

For some odd reason, though, it is not "Christianity" that Brown identifies as the culprit, the enemy of the true intentions of Jesus, but only the Catholic Church, consistently, and without exception. This, despite the fact that Orthodox and Protestant churches all affirm the divinity of Christ as defined by Nicaea and other early Church councils, all accept nearly the same canon of Scripture, and, in the case of Protestant churches that have diminished the role of Mary, the mother of Jesus, in their theology and practice, might merit criticism for banishing the "sacred feminine" from spirituality far more than Catholicism does.

So, for this reason, there might be a case for characterizing *The Da Vinci Code* as anti-Catholic. It's not just that Brown makes assertions (many of them) about Catholicism that are not true, but that he chooses to make the Roman Catholic Church guilty of crimes — misrepresenting Jesus, repressing the "sacred feminine," and rejecting the true leadership role of Mary Magdalene — for which, if you're going to follow his logic, all Christianity should be judged guilty.

Why did he do this? I suppose because it's simpler, that's why. That's the most charitable guess. It makes for easier writing and easier reading. Not more truthful writing, mind you, or writing that's more faithful to the complexities of real life and real history. For that would be a bit more difficult to do than pulling out stock villains in flowing robes, funny hats toting suitcases full of money.

So — according to *The Da Vinci Code*, Catholics are the only Christians?

Well, maybe, as I said, Catholics should be flattered.

We can probably understand if they're not.

For Further Reading

Catholic Christianity, by Peter J. Kreeft, Ignatius Press, 2001.

Questions for Review

1. What is Opus Dei?
2. How does *The Da Vinci Code* misrepresent the Christian world?

Questions for Discussion

1. What do you think the response of Christians should be to negative or mistaken portrayals of their faith in culture?
2. How do we view people who strive to live out the message of Jesus in the modern world?

epilogue

WHY IT MATTERS

If we had to find any good that's come out of *The Da Vinci Code* phenomenon, it's that it has stimulated a great deal of interest in important matters: who Jesus is, what early Christianity was all about, the power of art, and issues of gender and spirituality.

What's unfortunate is that the reading public has embraced the historical assertions made in *The Da Vinci Code* with such enthusiasm.

This enthusiasm betrays a failure of sorts — a failure of churches of all kinds to communicate these very basic facts of history and Christian theology to its members. The credulity with which readers have embraced Brown's assertions that early Christians did not see Jesus as divine, and the general implication that the form and content of Christianity are the consequences of nothing more than base power struggles, should be a wake-up call to all involved in ministry.

What are we teaching people about Jesus? Anything?

Stop Making Sense

Many readers have been disturbed by the assertions made about Christian faith they find in *The Da Vinci Code*. I hope this book has reassured you that faith in Jesus as Lord is organic and fundamental to the Christian faith, and has been since the first apostles set out to preach the Good News.

Let me make one final point to bring this out even more clearly.

A basic presumption of *The Da Vinci Code* is that the "winning" side of Christianity was dedicated to suppressing facts about Jesus that were uncomfortable, or unacceptable, or that it just didn't want out there.

Think for a moment about the illogic of this assertion. I've pointed out various aspects of this throughout the book, and it all, in the end, comes down to this:

What Brown defines as the "winning" and, we should emphasize, *false,* side of the Christian debate, suffered terribly for its assertions about Jesus.

Beginning, of course, with Jesus himself.

Think about it. If Jesus were nothing more than the gentle teacher of Brown's account, why would any authority bother to execute him? Why would they bother, as well, to crucify him, crucifixion being the method of execution reserved for the vilest, lowest criminals?

And if he were, indeed, just this teacher executed in this horrible manner, why would his followers abandon their normal, safe lives to spread his teaching, setting themselves up for a similar fate?

Moving on down the centuries, what's blindingly clear is that as Christians were arrested, tortured, and imprisoned, they were not, most definitely, being punished for following a philosopher. They were punished because, as Christianity was understood, they worshiped a God, embodied in Jesus of Nazareth, allegiance to whom prohibited them from honoring Caesar as lord or god. Their worldview, one in which God, through Jesus, reigned as Lord of the universe, was, quite frankly, a threat.

So our pursuit of logic takes us in two directions at this point.

First, although Brown says that early Christians didn't honor Jesus as Lord until Nicaea, we can see that if that were true, there would have been little reason to target them for persecution.

Second, if they really didn't believe Jesus was Lord, if underneath all of this language and liturgy proclaiming him to be, was a belief in just this mortal teacher, why didn't they just change their stories? If they didn't believe that Jesus was Lord, and that was the belief that was getting them thrown to the lions and exiled to the salt mines . . . why continue the ruse?

It simply makes no sense.

The point for us, as people interested in who Jesus really is and what Christianity believes about him, is this:

The whole *Da Vinci Code* scenario suggests that Christianity, as we know it, is a fabrication, and that the truth has been repressed. We have to think hard and logically about this. What benefit came to the apostles and early Christians to repress the truth? Did it bring them honor and praise? Did it make them rich? Did they gain power? Did what they proclaimed make their lives more comfortable and safer?

Would you go through what early Christians endured for something you knew to be a lie?

And, what happened to Jesus' body, anyway?

Meeting Jesus

I wrote this book because I wanted to help curious readers sort through the many interesting issues raised in *The Da Vinci Code*.

At the center of these issues stands not just an issue, but a person: Jesus of Nazareth. I'm convinced that the reason so many of us have embraced the claims of *The Da Vinci Code* with such credulity is because we've never seriously tried to get to know Jesus. Whether we are churchgoers or not, we've stood at a distance from him, letting others tell us what to think about him, never bothering to read even a single Gospel from beginning to end ourselves. And, in the end, we've absorbed the notion, so common in our culture, that it's all just a matter of opinion, anyway, with no sure truth at the heart of it.

Well, as the witness of the earliest apostles makes brilliantly clear, this is not about opinions, myths, or metaphors. Peter, Paul, and yes — Mary Magdalene — did not give their lives to a metaphor. They experienced Jesus as a human being, and, mysteriously, gloriously, as something more, and they gave their lives — literally — to him and the grace-filled, abundant life with which they were filled.

Any negative effect of *The Da Vinci Code* lies in the fact that in all the talk about Jesus and his wife, and the "sacred feminine," and in all the speculation about the "real story" — the Real Story is lost.

Jesus, crucified, died and risen, the One whose very real death and resurrection frees us from the power of our own very real sin and death, through whom creation and God are reconciled.

But then again, this story isn't really lost. It's not secret, either, and there's not a thing stopping any of us from discovering it.

Curious about Jesus?

The truth is as close as a book on your shelf.

And no, it's not *The Da Vinci Code.*

Don't let a novelist with an agenda instruct you in the ways of faith. Go back to the beginning, and go to the source: Pick up that Bible.

You might be surprised at what you find.

Our Sunday Visitor ...
Your Source for Discovering
the Riches of the Catholic Faith

Our Sunday Visitor has an extensive line of materials for young children, teens, and adults. Our books, Bibles, pamphlets, CD-ROMs, audios, and videos are available in bookstores worldwide.

To receive a FREE full-line catalog or for more information, call **Our Sunday Visitor** at **1-800-348-2440, ext. 3**. Or write **Our Sunday Visitor** / 200 Noll Plaza / Huntington, IN 46750.

Please send me ___ A catalog
Please send me materials on:
___ Apologetics and catechetics
___ Prayer books
___ The family
___ Reference works
___ Heritage and the saints
___ The parish

Name
Address _____ Apt._____
City _____ State _____ Zip_____
Telephone ( ) _____
                                                        A43BBBBP

Please send a friend ___ A catalog
Please send a friend materials on:
___ Apologetics and catechetics
___ Prayer books
___ The family
___ Reference works
___ Heritage and the saints
___ The parish

Name _____
Address _____ Apt._____
City _____ State _____ Zip_____
Telephone ( ) _____
                                                        A43BBBBP

OurSundayVisitor

200 Noll Plaza, Huntington, IN 46750
Toll free: **1-800-348-2440**
Website: www.osv.com